Fine

YEARS IN THE BUSINESS

Max Morath
THE ROAD TO RAGTIME

MAX MORATH

DIANE FAY SKOMARS

WITH

RALPH SCHOENSTEIN

The Donning Company/Publishers
184 Business Park Drive, Suite 106
Virginia Beach, VA 23462

Sally Davis, Associate Editor
Kelly M. Perkoski, Graphic Designer
John Harrell, Imaging Artist

Library of Congress Cataloging-in-Publication Data:

Morath, Max.
    Max Morath : the road to ragtime / Max Morath, Diane Fay Skomars :
with Ralph Schoenstein.
        p.   cm.
        Includes discography and a list of compositions.
        ISBN 1–57864–068–7 (alk. paper)
        1. Morath, Max. 2. Ragtime music—History and criticism.
        I. Skomars, Diane Fay. II. Schoenstein, Ralph, 1933–
        III. Title.

ML417. M86M67   1999
786.2' 1645'092—dc21
        [b]   99–19509
                                                                                  CIP

Printed in the United States of America

contents

"Lake Superior Couple" (Max & Diane).

My Introduction

Max Morath

Diane and I enjoy a minor disagreement about the contents of this book. She maintains it's a book about me, The Max. I say it is about *The Road*—my take on this land of ours after fifty years of touring out there in the entertainment business.

I can't imagine anyone except maybe my late mother and a few aging Colorado cronies showing interest in the cluttered resume of Max Morath—this hustler in the radio/TV dodges of mid-century, this erstwhile jazz sideman, jingle writer, earnest actor, so-so salesman, pretty good composer, accidental producer, late-blooming writer, and through it all, ragtime pianist. Can this aimlessly chaotic career be summed up as "Living a Ragtime Life?"

Well, yes.

The music called "ragtime" combines two things: chaos and discipline. The disciplined left hand provides a steady beat throughout, permitting wholesome chaos in the syncopating right. Ragtime, thus, becomes a metaphor for the life of the entertainer, at least for this one. To wit:

1. I've never been sure what the hell I was doing in show business.
   (Chaos.)

2. But I have always adhered to its cardinal rule. I show up.
   (Discipline.)

Showing up has meant chasing an audience, and against the odds, getting to the next gig on time, in saloons and music halls, theaters and TV shows—any of those inherently unstable operations. For a long time I thought that was my career, my life.

But then it dawned on me that my life is really *The Road*.

And I love it. The American Road is exciting and demanding and a joy all its own. I will grant you its occasional ugliness and dangers if you'll grant me its challenge and its comforts. It has led me to care for my country in a new and somewhat cockeyed way. I love the Bill of Rights, the Grand Canyon, and baseball, but

I've also fallen in love with our Interstate highways and our telephones, our truck stops and coffee shops. I cherish my credit cards; I consume fast food with complete faith in its uniformity across America; I treasure my stash of motel shampoo miniatures.

I'm lucky. As a performer playing the music of the past, I revel in the present, and relish the travels that take me, not only on to the next booking, but also into the American future. The Road is my never-ending adventure.

Diane Fay Skomars, my wife, has been a photographer all her life, and when she's on the Road with me, her camera naturally comes along. In shooting her husband's ragtime life she has also captured on film the theaters themselves, the stage crews, and the audiences in small towns and large.

At some point I said how about shooting my unending love affair with the Road itself, and since that time, for every image of me at a Road piano or of a stagehand focusing a spotlight, she has also captured my favorite icons on the Road—many of them signs and sights so familiar to most Americans that they seem like family portraits. These scenes have in turn inspired me to pass along, in essays and poems herein, some of my thoughts about life on the Road.

Thus Diane and I, happily married, solved that minor disagreement. Between the covers of this book we have married, quite happily, The Max and The Road.

My Introduction

Diane Fay Skomars
THE PHOTOGRAPHY

People ask me, "Do you play too?" My response is usually something like, "Would you cook if you were married to Craig Claiborne?"

However, Violet Glenn Alexander, my beloved childhood piano teacher in Duluth, billed me as her favorite pupil after Penny Yonkers graduated from high school. And she taught me to play the "Maple Leaf Rag" when I was twelve. Little did I know that I'd someday be sharing my life with the man who has spent years preserving the beauty of ragtime music. You can hear it played faster, slower, and more technically correct, perhaps, but you'll never hear it played sweeter.

Max and I first met in Duluth in 1964 at the university. I was a junior at UMD and he was performing at Kirby Student Center Ballroom. I remember him distinctly. He says he remembers me and that's sweet, but he doesn't.

However, we stayed in touch over the years. I found a career in higher education, and as my college or university brought him in to perform, I often helped with arrangements. As the years rolled on we shared infrequent lunches and annual holiday greetings, occasionally counseling each other through minor highs and lows. One spring, however, we met in New York. "Dinner and a show," he said. "I'll buy." That was that.

He wanted me to write about The Road, and how I was inspired by the American scene enough to love photographing highway markers and motel signs. Hogwash! That's his agenda. To me, the whole point of this book is Max.

So this book is for you, his fans. I've been a fan for some thirty-five years myself. From chatting with folks after the show, I know some of the questions you frequently ask about him. Here are my answers:

1. He was born in 1926.
2. Yes, he wrote and performed those programs on Public Television in the 1960s: "Ragtime Era" and "Turn of the Century."
3. No, they're not available on video cassette.
4. True, he is not single.

It's a "trip" traveling the USA with Max Morath, photographing his one-man show in theaters, town halls, and opera houses. And it has provided a good transition to my career in New York, where I have a studio of photography.

May you enjoy the following pages.

Living a Ragtime Life

"I think one reason people say musicians 'play' is that most of us never grow up."

"In America it's our **music** that labels our history, more than our wars, more **certainly** than our politicians . . ."

"It was a time when people were leaving the **farm** and going to the **city** so they could make enough money to move to the **country**."

"They said ragtime was a scurrilous music, reeking of excessive syncopations . . ."

". . . The greatest of them all was a quiet young black man from Texas by the name of Scott Joplin."

"I've never been sure at what point a folk song becomes a pop song. I think it's when it starts making money."

"Teddy Roosevelt loved ragtime. Woodrow Wilson didn't like it. Calvin Coolidge wouldn't say."

"Everything in America is ragtime, they talk in ragtime, "
It seems to be the fashion, their latest passion . . .

" . . . composers, just as thick as bees, "
writing raggy melodies . . .

" . . . let me take you to Alexander's grandstand, brass band, ain't you comin' along . . ."

"Got ragtime buddies and ragtime pals, Go to ragtime parties with ragtime gals . . ."

"The real American folk song is a rag, a mental jag,
A **tonic** for the chronic **blues** . . ."

"Ragtime happened to be the first new music that went national.

You heard the same tunes in New York that you did in San Francisco

and everywhere in between."

"Ragtime went out of style about the time of World War One, which in those days was called 'The Great War,'—just a working title until it was assigned a number."

"Millions of Americans went to the Chicago World's Fair and for the first time they saw two things: an electric light and a belly dancer. Long lines formed for both."

"... for the boys and girls it was still a world of innocence, no TV, no movies, no Internet to corrupt the kids. Just people."

The Entertainer

The Entertainer

By Ralph Schoenstein

The ideal thing for an artist to be is an original,

like Louis Armstrong, Pablo Picasso, Frank Sinatra, Dr. Seuss, or Max Morath. Of course, there is no one like any of these men, all but one household names. However, homey celebrity has never been the goal of a piano man named Max Morath. Max would probably tell you that another household name is Drano and still another used to be Lydia Pinkham's, a famous old American cure-all.

"A truly wonderful panacea," he likes to tell audiences. "Eighteen percent alcohol. Folks used to drink it to feel well enough to go to temperance meetings."

Max dispenses such enlightenment with a sly smile on a face craggy enough for Mount Rushmore. And he'd probably say that he would rather be part of the Catskills.

For the last fifty years, in all fifty states, Max Morath has been The Entertainer: a ragtime pianist, singer, humorist, and actor in the longest-running one-man show since William Jennings Bryan spent three decades running for President. And he is a household name in households that value the man who almost singlehandedly has fanned a love of ragtime in America.

Singlehandedly? No, he has played with two hands ever since boyhood, when he was taught piano by his

Ralph Schoenstein.

Long Beach, California, 1935:
Max, brother Fred, and mother
Gladys Ramsell Morath.

Colorado Springs High School, 1943: Left to right: Willis Griffee, Charles Morrow, Max, and Don Anderson.

mother, who played for silent films. In a land full of tacky trends and disposable fads, he has steadily been marching to a different drummer, for ragtime is a form of march. In a nation where fame sometimes lasts as long as six months and sometimes begins with a mug shot, Max Morath has spent half a century playing the music that charmed America from the Gay Nineties to World War I, our last carefree days, when germ warfare meant fighting a cold and ground zero was a Swedish weather report. From the time of the trouble in Korea to the time of the trouble in every place else, he has been America's premiere wandering minstrel, wandering for ten years longer than Moses but never in the wilderness, except for that stretch called Las Vegas.

This book is full of his love for both American music and the land that has made it.

Max has been a straw-hatted cheerleader for that land, not always an easy stance amidst all the growing cynicism here; but he is made of tough stuff, the stuff that was common when saloons suggested to their patrons, DON'T SHOOT THE PIANO PLAYER. HE'S DOING THE BEST HE CAN. Max's best has moved newspapers like the *San Francisco Chronicle* to say: "He is a consummate entertainer. His show is a surpassing delight on all levels— music, comedy, social history, sheer entertainment. He sings just enough and plays just enough and rambles just enough and displays the timing of a master without ever seeming slick. It is an extraordinary balance and an extraordinary show."

The Lone Ranger of radio used to ride in behind a voice that said, "Return with us now to those thrilling days when the West was young." The Lone Arranger of Ragtime walks to a piano for a message that says: *Return with me now to what you think was a happier turn of the century*. He has spent five decades cheerfully catering to what one critic called "that ache we all have for lost times, when the sun was warmer, the days and nights longer, and everything was cozy and safe."

It was exactly one hundred years ago that Americans suddenly fell in love with a piece called the "Maple Leaf Rag" by the black genius, Scott Joplin. Max, a zealous researcher,

Nightclubbing in San Francisco, 1945: Max with father Fred P. Morath, brother Fred R. Morath.

says the word "rag" probably evolved from nineteenth-century black culture as a reference to songs outside gospel music. Played by itinerant pianists, these songs became pieces called "rags," which soon became "ragtime" and meant a specific piece of syncopated music. Decades later, writer E. L. Doctorow used Ragtime to define the entire era.

Unfortunately, the "Maple Leaf Rag" was the only hit of Joplin's lifetime. However, the rag did trigger something uniquely wonderful: To thousands of upright pianos went the sheets of a new American music that hadn't been imported from the stages of Italy or the beer gardens of Bavaria, music sometimes leisurely, sometimes uptempo, and always more complex than "Yankee Doodle" or "Home Sweet Home."

In a land full of tacky trends and disposable fads, he has steadily been marching to a different drummer, for ragtime is a form of march.

"In ragtime piano," says Max in a Western voice for which a microphone is superfluous, "there are three or four phrases of sixteen measures in duple time, with the left hand keeping a steady march-like beat and the right hand constantly syncopating against it."

Understanding ragtime from those words is like knowing the Taj Mahal from a set of its plans. There are no words to capture the essence of any music, for music has always transcended language: the fat lady breaks into song when words will no longer do.

And fat ladies happened to be the pinups of the Ragtime Era, their beefy beauty reflecting the fat and supposedly contented country of the years from 1890 to 1915.

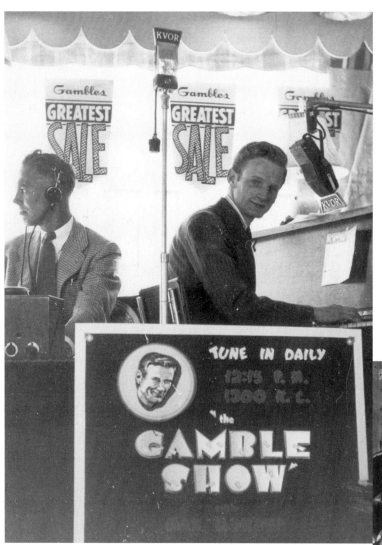

LEFT:
Colorado Springs, 1946: live radio broadcast from the window of Gamble's; Engineer H. Cozine "Cozy" Strang at left.

RIGHT:
Broadcasting live coverage of annual AdAmAn New Year's Eve fireworks from Air Force C-47, Colorado Springs, 1947.

"It was a time when sex was dirty and the air was clean," says Max in the voice of the witty historian whose commentary salts *The Road to Ragtime.*

As Stephen Holden of *The New York Times* said of this show: "It's a seamless blending of vintage pop music—played, sung, and occasionally danced by Mr. Morath—interwoven with artfully chosen tidbits of Americana. Seated at a grand piano under a Tiffany lamp, and flanked by an Edison phonograph, the musicologist, storyteller, and expert in turn-of-the-century Americana seems the very epitome of an old-time vaudevillian. But in reflecting with humor on our longing for "the good old days," Mr. Morath is much more than a devoted nostalgist. He is a philosopher of American popular culture with Mark Twain's gift of gab and farsighted historical view. The picture he paints is of a world we might want to visit but almost certainly wouldn't want to live there."

There are no words to capture the essence of any music, for music has always transcended language . . .

"Yes," says Max, "in spite of the enchanting music, it was a tough time to live. Most people didn't do anything but work and die. 'A cozy time?' that critic said. Well many of those cozy people died of diphtheria at twelve."

And, of course, as Max says, sex wasn't invented until 1915.

"No, I'm not a nostalgia vendor," says Max. "I've always thought nostalgia sounded like something to rub on your chest: 'Just apply a little Nostalgia, Mrs. Morath, and the boy will stop wheezing.' And I don't believe in 'the good old days' either. They don't exist, except in rose-colored memory. When folks my age

The view of Pikes Peak, New Year's Eve, 1947; AdAmAn club was founded by Fred and Ed Morath, Max's father and uncle.

talk about 'the good old days,' they're talking about the Depression. I wonder if the Spaniards in 1600 got wistful about the Inquisition and Englishmen in 1700 went weepy over the black plague."

"There are, however, two things from my own good old days that I do sorely miss: steam-driven train travel and a decent chocolate malt. Lamenting the loss of train travel has been overdone, although I have to say this for trains: I never sat in one for three hours circling the depot. And a decent chocolate malt in these days of undrinkable semi-liquid ice cream—finding one has been my search for the syrupy holy grail. I trace the decline of Western civilization from the moment that the first misguided counterman put in that first squirt of Cool Whip."

Ironically, in spite of being anti-nostalgia, Max keeps visiting the wonderful-awful time from 1890 to 1915 because "it was the beginning of everything: the movies, Corn Flakes, phonographs, aspirin, disposable razor blades, standard time, automatic weapons, mass magazines, and consistently successful appendec-

tomies. What you had in those years was progress and optimism, ending in the disillusionment of the war."

The ragtime tunes are bewitching, but the big breakthrough was in the words of the songs, for they captured the distinctive American idiom of the time. However, by the early 1900s, these words stopped making sense. "When Ragtime Rosie Ragged the Rosary" is not a song about cutting up at mass: it's merry nonsense by Edgar Leslie and Lewis F. Muir.

Meanwhile, a far better composer, Irving Berlin, was writing "Everything in America is Ragtime." Berlin, says Max, was the first composer to write syncopated inner rhymes. Although Joplin had only the one ragtime hit, Berlin had many and they were much livelier than the cool Joplin rags. This Russian immigrant caught the mood of his new home with such thoughts as,

In those days, nobody cared if Rosie ragged the rosary or Sheldon shimmied the shul.

> Musical demon, set your honey a-dreamin'
> Won't you play me some rag.
> Just change that classical nag
> To some sweet beautiful drag.

What is a classical nag? Beethoven's horse? And what is beautiful drag? A transvestite in Calvin Klein? In those days, nobody cared if Rosie ragged the rosary or Sheldon shimmied the shul.

Max Morath has been playing some rag since the days when Harry Truman was playing White House gigs; but his reputation was slow to grow because, as *The Coloradoan* said, "He is difficult to categorize." Americans—both audiences and critics—respond fastest to talents that can be pigeonholed. For example, Duke Ellington, one of the greatest American composers of the twentieth century, never won a Pulitzer Prize because he was beyond category.

He is a philosopher of American popular culture with Mark Twain's gift of gab and farsighted historical view.

In the spirit of Ellington, Max Morath has never stopped following his star, even though at times it has seemed more like Hale-Bopp than Venus; but an original always insists that the public come to him. He will not allow a record company to make him sing "Candle in the Wind" or "Doggie in the Window."

It was fitting that an echo of the ragtime era, "Yes, We Have No Bananas," was one of the hits when Max Morath was born in Colorado Springs on October 1, 1926. His arrival was aided by a country doctor and land speculator, who told Max's father to tell the boy, "Never put your money into anything you can't piss on," a philosophical flight that probably wasn't taught at Yale.

Max's two great loves, American music and the American land, are traceable to his parents. Gladys Ramsell was an Iowa woman who

knew that Brahms' "Lullaby" didn't swing, so she played ragtime piano for her two sons, Max and Frederic, while supporting them as the landlady of a rooming house, as an accountant, and then, for twenty-five years, as the society editor of the *Colorado Springs Gazette-Telegraph*. Her income enabled Max's father, Frederic Palmer Morath, to devote most of his time to not making a living. A vagabond whose first love was the outdoors, Frederic went out of his way to pass up employment so he could wander in the mountains, spending much more time with the peaks than with his progeny.

"I hardly knew him," says Max, "but from what I did know, my dad was a lovely man."

LEFT:
Imperial Hotel, Cripple Creek, Colorado, 1950; pianist and musical director for melodrama, "Lily, the Felon's Daughter."

RIGHT:
Cripple Creek Barbershop Quartet, 1950; Left to right: Max, Don Dorrell, Tom Rea, and Milt Commons.

ABOVE &
UPPER RIGHT:
On camera, KKTV,
1953–1954.
LOWER RIGHT:
Production Manager KKTV,
Colorado Springs/Pueblo,
1953–1954.

KKTV show "Shopping Notes," with Norma Loy Tackitt, 1952; Max and Norma were married in 1953.

In 1933, Franklin D. Roosevelt told Americans to be optimistic and seven-year-old Max responded by taking piano lessons.

"But I never studied seriously," he says, "and some music critics have agreed."

A typically self-effacing thought from a man whose piano playing leaves nothing to be desired but an encore, a man with a first rate technique for everything from Joplin to Johnny Mercer.

Four years later, Max broke into broadcasting by winning a radio talent contest with imitations of both Popeye and Donald Duck, impressively unveiling a two-species mouth. Unfortunately, the demand for imitators of morons and ducks was limited, so Max intensified his piano study, learning the "Maple Leaf Rag" by the time he was twelve.

At sixteen, when he was in high school, Max began writing musical arrangements while studying composition and theory and also singing in barbershop quartets. He worked his way through Colorado College, where he got a degree in English; and by the time of his graduation, he was both playing jazz gigs and doing radio announcing. For the next five years, he was a Rocky Mountain Renaissance man who played piano, sang, acted, wrote, and produced; and in 1952, he moved into TV, where he wrote, announced, edited, acted, and sang at Colorado's new KKTV.

At twenty-six, Max Morath was an Orson Welles with a good left hand.

In the early 1950s, Max began playing ragtime in the saloons of Cripple Creek, Colorado. In 1953, the year that he married actress Norma Loy Tackitt, he made his first recording, which was simultaneously issued on 33, 45, and 78 rpms. It sold in equally small amounts at all three speeds; perhaps Max needed a new one. In 1954, Americans were turning to rock. Ragtime had all the appeal of Offenbach's Greatest Hits.

> At twenty-six, Max Morath was an Orson Welles with a good left hand.

After a couple of years of playing in clubs and restaurants, and also writing commercials, ballads, and even ragtime of his own, Max was feeling no Rocky Mountain high from his versatility.

"When I hit thirty," he says, "I thought once a week of quitting the business."

The business might not have known.

The "Gramercy Ghost."

Acting in Civic Theater Productions,
mid-1950s, directed by Orvis I. Grout.
RIGHT:
"The Fourposter," with Gwen Stout.
BELOW LEFT:
"Detective Story;" Max at left.

In rehearsal and production for PBS television, "The Ragtime Era," and "Turn of the Century;" KRMA-TV Denver, 1960–1961.

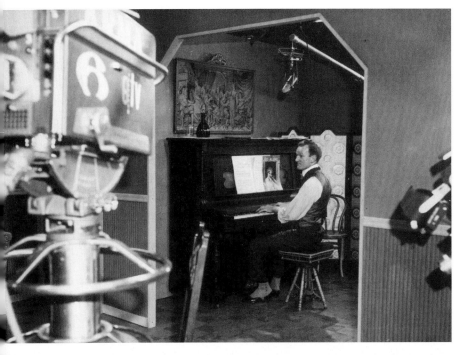

Kansas Centennial, State
Fairgrounds, Topeka, 1961.

However, in spite of an income that at times was a busboy's, Max persevered and began to concentrate more on performing, composing, singing, and recording ragtime piano. By 1959, he had played Cripple Creek Imperial Hotel melodramas for almost a decade. Cripple Creek was hardly Salzburg, but playing there was better than serving hamburgers, although Max did that too for a couple of weeks, wondering if Irving Berlin had ever said, "Do you want fries with that?"

And then, early in 1960, the singing waiter was suddenly recognized by more than his family: He was hired by PBS to write and perform twelve half-hour shows on the Ragtime Era to be broadcast in the fall. At the same time he began to take his one-man show to American colleges and he also did national commercials for Beechnut Peppermint Gum, which Van Cliburn had never been able to get.

The success of Max's Ragtime Era moved PBS to have him do two new series: one about cowboys and one about life at the turn of the

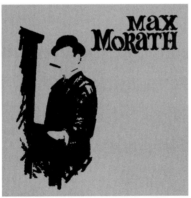

century. By 1963, Max had a Columbia Records contract, was performing at New York's Blue Angel, and was able to get out of gum. The following year, he and Norma, who now had two daughters and a son, moved to New York City, where Max's new Original Rag Quartet played the Village Vanguard that summer; and then the quartet went on the road with Dinah Shore, who was as explosively upbeat as Max. The two of them made Pat Boone sound cranky.

In the summer of 1968, after three years of concerts, club dates, recordings, and Arthur Godfrey's radio show, Max spent seven weeks in Durango, Colorado, where he broke in his new one-man theatrical, "Max Morath at the Turn of the Century."

In the early seventies, while also making records and appearing on TV, Max never stopped touring with this show, which had more than eight hundred performances. In the middle of that decade, he began touring with a new show, "The Ragtime Years"; and he followed "The Ragtime Years" with "One for the Road," the story of America's love affair with alcohol and drugs. "One for the Road," however, turned out to be a show that almost drove Max himself to the bottle: the reviews were as mixed as the drinks and audiences seemed to prefer alcohol and drugs to the show. Because people wanted only Max's musical highs, the show did not survive.

. . . the quartet went on the road with Dinah Shore, who was as explosively upbeat as Max. The two of them made Pat Boone sound cranky.

Now affiliated with Columbia Artists Management, Max returned to the more appealing intoxication of music and formed a quintet for a new show called "Pop!! Goes the Music: American Music and How It Got That Way," a long lilting history lesson. After opening at New York's Michael's Pub, the show then toured for three years, to reviews that said Max was "a prodigious talent" and "America's Music Man for all seasons." Those were fitting words, for Max does have the commanding charm of Professor Harold Hill. He could probably sell you some land to piss on and then find an old song for it.

By the mid-eighties, America's Music Man was strutting to wide acclaim. His new one-man show, "Living a Ragtime Life," opened Off-Broadway to fine reviews in 1986 and Max then took it around a country he had gotten to know like the back of his syncopating hand,

Whenever asked, "How did you find ragtime?" he replies, "Ragtime found me . . ."

In "Ragtime Revisited," touring 1962–1966.

the country so elegantly celebrated in this book. Moreover, his recording of his own composition, *The Cripple Creek Suite: A Ragtime Suite for Piano*, was showing Americans that there was one other form of native music besides jazz that they should treasure.

Never resting long on old material about the old days, Max created still new material about the old days in a fourth show, "The Ragtime Man," with which he began touring in the early nineties after five years of "Living a Ragtime Life." He was, however, also exploring other roads; and in 1996 at Columbia University, he earned a master's degree in American Studies, with a thesis called "Three Songs: The Life and Work of Carrie Jacobs Bond." Moreover, Max now was looking ahead to life with someone even more educated than he: with Diane Fay Skomars, a university administrator and photographer, who became his wife in 1993. Her artistry is the heart of this book.

"These pictures celebrate a country that still works," says Diane, "a country that still feels good about itself. America is precious to Max and me and we truly love meeting its people as they come to hear him perform. Many of them enter the theater looking tired and cranky. But they go out holding hands. And when Max plays his slow rags—and those are his sweetest songs—I can see these people melt."

Max, of course, began doing such heartwarming work in American studies long before he went to Columbia; and he has never stopped savoring America's past with both irony and melodious joy.

Whenever asked, "How did you find ragtime?", he replies, "Ragtime found me," a connection that has filled him with a supremely contagious delight for the last fifty years. He remembers E. L. Doctorow's words about the Ragtime Era: "A certain light was still available." And this happy piano man plans to keep reflecting that light long after the new century's turn.

ABOVE:
Onstage with the Original Rag Quartet, 1964; Max and (left to right): James Tyler, Barry Kornfeld, and Felix Pappalardi.

The
ORIGINAL
RAG
QUARTET
WITH MAX MORATH

BELOW:
Singing "Mr. Gallagher
and Mr. Shean" with Burl
Ives; NBC's "Bell
Telephone Hour," 1966.

Guesting on TV's "Dinah!" 1967. Left to right: Max, Gary Owens, Dinah, Marcel Marceau, Zsa Zsa Gabor, and Mike Neun.

Jan Hus Theater, New York, 1969;
One-Man show "Max Morath at the
Turn of the Century."

For Max Morath
a great performer, a great philosopher,
a great American and a nice man!
Arthur Godfrey
6/14/73

With Arthur Godfrey, New York, 1973.

"Composers' Showcase" Concert, Whitney Museum, New York, 1972. Left to right: Willie "The Lion" Smith, Eubie Blake, Earl "Fatha" Hines, Dir. Charles Schwartz, William Bolcom, and Max.

On tour with one-man show
"The Ragtime Years,"
1973–1978.

BELOW:
Mendota, Minnesota
Emporium of Jazz, circa 1981;
with Butch Thompson, clarinet.

LEFT:
Recording at Vanguard Studios,
New York, 1976.

BELOW:
KET Television, Lexington,
Kentucky, 1976; video-taping
GED Grammar Project.

Quartet in "One for the Road," Left to right: Max, Peter Walker, Davis Gaines, and Gerold Quimby.

Original revue "One for the Road," St. Louis Repertory Theater, 1982; with Peter Walker and Carol Morley.

On tour with "Pop Goes the Music," 1984; Left to right: Max, Howard Alden, Chuck Wilson, Don Haviland, and Chuck Spies.

Touring the U.S.A., 1999.

With his best friend, Jordan Bayless (d. 1998;) at video-
taping performances, Denver Media Center, 1992.

Graduating from Columbia University, New York.
May, 1996. Master's Degree, American Studies.

As "The Ragtime Man," the one-man show on tour, 1998.

Max's daughter KATHY MORATH is an actress, singer, writer and director, and proud wife and mother. She currently lives in Dallas, Texas.

CHRISTY MAINTHOW is Max's daughter, the devoted mother of David and Eric, and wife of advertising and marketing executive Michael Mainthow. She also does TV commercials and models for the Ford Agency in New York.

FRED MORATH, Max's son, lives in Kailua, Hawaii with his wife Paula Jacobs Morath and their daughter, Malia. He is a tradesman, painter and carpenter, actor, and voice-over master.

MONETTE MAGRATH, daughter of Diane Fay Skomars, is an actress and a recent graduate of New York University's Tisch School of the Arts. She lives in Hollywood with her cat, Olive.

Cruising Altitude

Cruising Altitude

Three Letter Words

Three Letter Words
Three Letter Words
Three Letter Words

I like it when words from the airline computer
Appear on the tag when I check my two-suiter:
FAR is for Fargo and Fresno is FAT,
SEA is Seattle 'cause that's where it's at.
Oakland is OAK, that's a logical bit,
Like Yuma is YUM and Pittsburgh is PIT,
ELM is Elmira and Allentown ABE,
While Daytona Beach, for the rhyme, must be DAB.

Who dreamed up these names? Philadelphia's PHL?
Milwaukee's MKE or perhaps Billings BIL?
JAN down in Jackson (a he or a she?)
Or FLO out in Florence, I think in S-C.
And don't call it LAX, it's pronounced L-A-X,
Though Mexico City's okay to call MEX,
Jacksonville's JAX and Lexington's LEX,
And Portland, for some reason's, called P-D-X.
Canadian airports all start with a Y,
Though no one in Canada's figured out why.
Montreal is a Y, plus an M and an X,
Which brings me to close with a note about sex.
Never make jokes about Sioux city (SUX)
If you're flying from there down to Phoenix, or PHX.

The Read

If you're a seasoned air traveler, chances are you have a Read going. Your book is probably a paperback, maybe it's a hard-cover crammed into your carry-on, but even discounted at Barnes & Noble, a hardcover is a major investment. And if you forget when boarding to extract this bulky Read from your carry-on, you may have trouble getting at it once you're airborne. It's probably blocked in the overhead by diaper bags, camera cases, and massive canvas wardrobe fold-overs that should have been checked but never are. No, the Well-Tempered Traveler awaits the paperback editions, themselves now painfully pricey. But you must have a Read. Otherwise your choices aloft will be the movie (*Animal House IV*,) articles in the airline magazine ("Pet Care," "Municipal Bonds," "Tofu,") or heavy drinking.

It must not rip the pocket, squish the book, or cause discomfort upon sitting.

Follow Morath's Law (ML) on paperbacks. Although the Law has kept me from traveling with certain authors whom I admire, including Stephen King, Robert Ludlum, and the late James Michener, it has in compensation provided me with considerable savings in clothing costs and comfort aloft. ML dictates that the PB (Paper-Back or Pocket Book, as they were first known) must fit in the rear left-side pants pocket (for right-side wallet folks.) It must not rip the pocket, squish the book, or cause discomfort upon sitting. These parameters unfortunately eliminate the mega-novelists above, but provide guidance and challenge in your search for a good Read. You must select first-rate *thin* books.

One of the great traumas of air travel, right up there with engine failure and unopenable peanut packages, is forgetting your Read when you deplane. If you must put it in the seat pocket in front of you when napping or munching, position it to stick out considerably, using a vomit bag to mark your place and to draw your eye to it upon deplaning. I once walked off a Northwest 737 with thirty unread pages in one of John D. MacDonald's Travis McGee novels. There was no replacement at that airport's bookshop, so I tracked down two maintenance workers who had serviced the aircraft. They claimed they couldn't find my Read, and I believed them. But I realized that the folks who clean and prep the airliners are among the most literate of Americans. They told me they retrieve as many as ten books per working day. It would be snobbish, I suppose, to regret that they're not walking away with Faulkner and Melville, but that's a result of our taste, not theirs. At least they're getting plenty of Grisham, Steele, Schoenstein, and an occasional John Irving. The typical Well-Tempered Traveler, remember, has invested in escape, not angst, and does not expect to become a better person as a result of the Read.

It's deceptively easy to abandon a Read. You're at 37,000 feet, basking in that delicious gift of free time a journey by air provides you. Drowsy, you ram your Read deep into the seat pocket in front of you. Could you forget it? No way. Not a Travis McGee novel. (All twenty of them, by the way, are perfect pocket-fitters.) You'll finish it tonight at the motel.

You are shocked awake as the airplane touches down. The lights flash on, and the passengers, as one, shift into deplane mode. They know they can't get off yet, but they act like someone in Row 40 has just yelled fire. You have no choice and join the panic. On your feet in the crush, you can't recall where you stuffed your three carry-ons. (You're supposed to have only one but you cheated.) Then the elderly gentleman across the aisle asks if you would help pull down his portmanteau, and as you do, the two-year-old in the seat ahead spills his apple juice on his dad's laptop, and you try to help out by sponging up the flood with an airline pillow. Behind you (you're in 8-D; the Well-Tempered Traveler always requests aisles forward) the surge of supercharged passengers reaches riot size and you are swept along. Rushed and flushed, you grab your stuff and stagger off to Terminal B.

Too late. By the time you discover you left your Read in the seat pocket, it's on its way to Sioux Falls. Maintenance or the next Traveler in 8-D gets it, while you scramble to the airport's book shop, desperate for another copy so you can finish your prized Read. You won't find it, of course, but you'll pay anything—*anything*!

Want an idea for making big bucks on books? I may just try it someday. I've set up a kiosk in the middle of, say, the United Terminal at O'Hare. You've just deplaned and walk by. I buy the paperback you just finished for a dollar, and sell it for two dollars later that day. You've made a buck and had a good Read; the next traveler saves about $5.00 and gets a new Read, prime but for a few dog-ears and a spot or two of yogurt or black coffee. Everybody wins. I'll bet I could turn $500 per day with an hour off for lunch.

So someday if my ragtime hustle wanes and my bookings wither, look for me at ORD, JFK, maybe LAX. I'll be operating my low overhead, high-profit booth, "Reads Only." (Working title) Other possibilities: Need-a-Read, The Book Stops Here, Road Readers, Reader Rotor. . . .

The Ride

  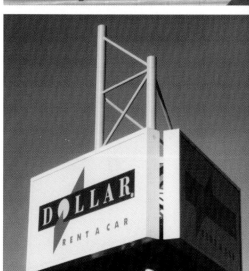

The Ride

Avis is red, Thrifty is blue,
  Budget and Alamo use colors two;

    Hertz, black and yellow
  (Most often seen),

    Dollar's a rainbow,
  National's green.

The Road

The Road

There are hazards great when it's getting late
And the miles are dragging by;
Your body moans and your engine groans
And you think they both will die;
The road beneath is a narrow sheath
Where the semis sway and whine.
You're low on gas and afraid to pass
On the double yellow line.

You were told this two-lane road
Was fast and smooth and pretty.
Someone lied; the one you've tried
Is slow and rough and gritty.
It curves and bumps by city dumps,
By Super-, K-, and Walmarts,
You're dodging kids and garbage lids
And drifting A&P carts.

A dog-eared map is on your lap,
Your road's in faded blue,
You slow for lights and flick your brights
And stop and start and stew.
You need to eat, you're tired, you're beat,
Afraid you'll simply fold,
And even worse, to match your thirst
Your bladder starts to scold.

Your fuel is nil, on every hill
Your engine kicks and pops,
You've only got a mile or so
Before the damned thing stops.
You're on the fumes, disaster looms
The night is cold and mean,
But up ahead in double red,
The map shows I-15!

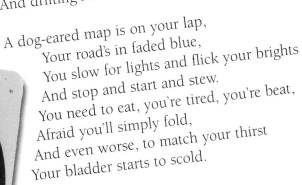

The Interstate, the Interstate, it's coming into view,
Just in time there'll be a sign in red and white and blue,
You'll set your Cruise, tune in the news, and find a Cluster, too,
The Interstate, the Interstate, the road that's really two!

he Interstate was put together piece by piece, beginning in the mid-1950s. Land was acquired and construction completed in short stretches. For miles you white-knuckled in the accepted practice of risking your life on a twisting, high-speed two-lane road. Then, Glory! Up ahead you saw those gracious green and white signs welcoming you to a new piece of I-70 or I-35. (Even numbers east-west, we learned, odd north-south.) Speed limits: maximum 70, minimum 40. Cruise control was already on the drawing boards in Detroit.

Underpinning our Interstate euphoria was the realization, however subconscious, that on an I-road you would probably not die in a head-on. You might nod off and ram a bridge abutment, or blow a tire and catapult over a guard-railed embankment, but no longer did oncoming drivers, casually aiming their vehicles to miss yours by a margin of six feet, hold your life in their hands, like during those countless crucial moments on the old two-laners.

Since time began, a "road" (street, lane, path, pike, track, by-way, avenue) ran both ways. A traveler on foot, on a horse, behind an ox-cart, passed another traveler going the opposite direction with a howdy or a glare, little more.

Then came the horseless carriage, the automobile, the truck, the van, the SEMI! Old ways die hard. Within a dozen or so years we found ourselves playing the Road version of Russian Roulette, hoping to pass and miss without damage, not a hiker or a horse, but masses of metal and glass rocketing toward each other at combined speeds up to 150 miles per hour, piloted by individuals with nothing in common but velocity and determination. At the critical moment of missing me—I refuse to call it passing—they could be reading, dozing, talking on their cellphone, drinking a beer, or trying to tune in NPR. *Whoosh!* Success. We

miss! But next time? At night? In snow? Stoned?

It was the builders of either the elegant Westside Highway in New York, or the celebrated Pennsylvania Turnpike who first addressed this madness. Why not, said some nameless civil engineer, build four lanes instead of two, and divide them? And while we're at it, let's eliminate cross traffic, doing away with millions of other daily possibilities to kill and maim. The seeds of the Interstate System were sown.

In the late '40s futurists were assured Oohs and Aahs when they informed Americans that we'd soon be driving from New York to San Francisco without a stoplight. Their predictions came true years ago and I don't think the nation took any notice at all. We should have thrown a party. When the transcontinental railroaders connected in 1869, a golden spike was driven in Utah and the country went bananas; when the first telephone call was made from New York to San Francisco, songs and poems were written and "Hello, Frisco" events went on for weeks.

I worry over the state of the Interstate as I would for friend or family. Are its potholes being filled? Is it getting enough funding? Should it have its bridges checked? The Interstates have made life on the road so much safer and simpler that for travelers like me they have become old pals. And we know the system like we know our blood type and our phone number.

On tour a few years ago somewhere out West, my stage manager and I found ourselves with a few days off around Thanksgiving, the next show scheduled the following week in Ohio. He'd take the car and drive up to see his folks in Minneapolis. I'd fly home and meet him next week in Akron. I asked him how he planned to reach the Twin Cities. "Simple," he said. "You just go to Kansas City and turn left."

Oh Engineers!
I sing your Divided Highway,
Your graceful Cloverleaf,
Embrace your Merge and Exit Only.
I Do Not Enter thoughtlessly.
In green and white
Signs, I know the light of freedom
Shines, and hope,
By keeping to my right
Of cheating bloody fate.
Oh, Blessed Interstate.

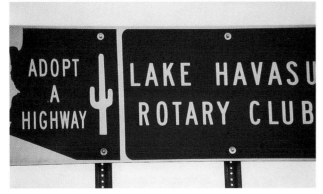

Clusters

Clusters

A Cluster is action and color and sass,
A Cluster has telephones, toilets, and gas,
    Burgers and shakes and a pizza to go,
A Cluster has comfort, convenience, and class.

You may have another name for them. I call them "Clusters."

As the Interstate Highway system grew, new intersections were created. Limited access did away with old crossroads and their mom-and-pop motels, one-pump gas stations and general stores. But motorists, more than ever, needed food, toilets, beds, phones, soda pop, beer, and cigarettes.

So Clusters, like gardens, grew at the new intersections.

A Cluster is not a town.

It is not a "Service Area" which is a sealed-access food/fuel/pit stop on a toll road, necessary but charmless, its vast restrooms recalling dormitory life. Or prison.

A Cluster is not planned, it happens. No single company or service designed it or dominates it.

A Cluster has no name, although it is in many respects a village—a new kind of village absolutely in the NOW, constantly changing.

No two Clusters are the same in size or content.

The Cluster is an Oasis for Modern Man and Women, the traveler's Hidey-Hole.

Clusters are not to be found at the intersection of two Interstates. There, high speed exit ramps and guard-railed cloverleafs have consumed the prime chunks of real estate suitable for a Texaco or a Wendy's. No, the ideal Cluster forms itself at the intersection of an Interstate with a U.S. highway, or with a state highway of sizable traffic flow.

A Cluster is not planned, it happens.

A Cluster must contain at least two of the following: service stations; fast-food drive-ins; budget motels; "Family" restaurants, e.g., Denny's, Shoney's, Perkin's, which are NOT counted as fast-fooders; a decent number of pay telephones; accessible restrooms. A great agony of The Road in our time is that service stations, formerly "gas" stations which now sell mostly food, beer, and prophylactics, are eliminating toilets. And even if they do have a biffy, you have to wade through acres of merchandise to reach it, so you feel guilty and purchase a Snickers or a Coors to justify your use of it.

Many Clusters contain a Truck Stop. Don't be intimidated by the eighteen-wheelers with their rumbling diesels and their pony-tailed and pot-bellied drivers. Truck drivers are hard working men and women, and are never a threat. They are too tired. Good food is always available at the Truck Stop—heavy stuff with lots of grease and sugar and caffeine, the big needs for the long haul. Truck stops have showers, too, and banks of pay phones and audiotapes—mostly country music. Truckers hate rock. Truck stops are often positioned alone—at a major intersection, but a lonely one. The timid four-wheeled traveler will probably pass on by, looking for a Mega-Cluster, or at least a Mini.

Clusters shout their welcome in red and yellow, blue and orange

Yes, Clusters fall into one of three categories: the Mini, the Maxi, and the Mega. Some Minis just barely reach Cluster status, sporting a lone McDonald's across from a Phillips 66, with maybe a Taco Bell under construction. This is not yet a valid Cluster, but may be seen as a Mini in gestation. A full-fledged Mini will offer the above minimums, thus the name.

The Maxi Cluster, you'd guess, is my favorite, not only because we share the name, but also because it offers ultimate succor to a man on The Road; it is the weary traveler's boon. It submits choices: the Ramada or the Motel 6; the Burger King or the Sizzler sit-down. And somewhere amidst the Maxi you can find alcohol in its civil varieties. Good food is at the same table, of course, but a couple of beers

> ... when you shut off your engine, you shut off your anxieties.

(always try the local and regional brands), a wine or even a whisky are OK. You're headed for your Super 8 and a hot tub.

The Maxi Cluster works wonders on levels deeper than the needs of your car and your carcass. It speaks of serenity and safety. You've never seen it before and probably never will again, but you're confident of its pleasures. There are no surprises, no price gouges or dirty sheets or sour mayo. (Well, hardly ever.) You have entered the kingdom of the Cluster, and when you shut off your engine, you shut off your anxieties.

No one plans a Cluster. The highway engineers hadn't a clue that clusters would blossom like wildflowers along their Interstates, or that

> Their bright colors enchant the child in you as you round a final curve at dusk, and behold the lush garden of a Cluster intersection.

their dearest attribute would indeed be that of wildflowers: color. Clusters shout their welcome in red and yellow, blue and orange. Their bright colors enchant the child in you as you round a final curve at dusk, and behold the lush garden of a Cluster intersection.

I worry that someday Clusters will be incorporated, given names, even Zip Codes. Some already bear titles, mainly those on the toll roads in the East: the Theodore Dreiser on the Indiana Turnpike; the Edison on the New Jersey; the Governor this or Senator that on the New York Thruway. Next thing a Cluster will think it's a town, elect a mayor and a city council, levy taxes.

Observe the fate of the Mega, the third and final member of the Cluster family. Its growth became cancerous; it is indeed on its way to becoming, God forbid, a city, and is to be avoided. It brings not serenity and safe harbor, but heartburn and parking fees. A Mega is, simply put, too much. The big hotels have arrived—a Sheraton, a Hilton. They book conventions, and thicken the traffic; an eight-screen Cinema attracts honking teens and grumpy seniors who overflow the booths at Shoney's. Then some developer decides what a great place for a shopping center and the Wal/K-Mart types move in. You're looking at terminal suburban sprawl, with an Office Max or a Home Depot waiting over at the County Courthouse for a zoning variance and a building permit.

But if you do have to stop at a Mega, don't fail to exploit certain of its unique advantages:

1. Check into a Motel 6 or any budget, and the next morning put on a coat and tie, walk over to the Hyatt or Marriott, and scarf down a free continental breakfast.

2. Hang around as if you're waiting for the maid to make up your king-size suite and use the house fax and copier. You're comfortable, and have saved time looking for a Kinko's.

3. Wear your swim trunks under your suit and hit the pool before the SUVs disgorge the four o'clock check-ins and they grab all the lounge chairs.

4. Use the house phones to book a budget motel for the next night at a perfect Cluster you found on the hotel's computer at *www.maxicluster.com* (some of us are working on it). Thank the desk clerk for a pleasant stay, and hit The Road.

In Kansas or Georgia or
South of Duluth,

Near Philly or
Dallas or Minot,

For burgers, and gas
and a telephone booth,

When a Cluster appears,
you'll say, "Why not?"

Since this book is about an Entertainer on the Road, these verses about the Road may be sung to the tune of Scott Joplin's "The Entertainer."

At a Cluster of any size
Fill up on sodas and burgers and fries.
Use the biffy and top your tank,
Get a Malt, and some cash at a bank.
Then arrive at a Motel Six
In your pickup or yellow Rolls-Royce,
Or a Rodeway or Sleep Inn, or just take a peep in
A Hyatt or Hilton or Choice.

Boston Market, Ramada, Hess,
A Hampton Inn and a Chicken Express.
Roy Rogers and Budgetel,
Or a room at a major hotel.
If the Sheraton says they're booked,
Call up the HoJo or Embassy Suites.
Stop at Arbie's or Denny's or Hardee's or Wendy's
For newspapers, coffee, and eats.

Never mind if you're running late,
You're guaranteed at a new Super 8.
Need a nacho? Perhaps a beer?
You can bet there's an Applebees near;
And McDonald's or KFC,
A Steak and Ale, a DQ, a BP,
Or an Amoco, Conoco, Texaco, Shell,
What a Cluster this turned out to be!

Finding the Bluebird

Finding the Bluebird

S ome Bluebirds are called simply "Cafe" or "Eat." "Rainbow" is another generic: "The Rainbow Cafe and Grill." But I call the local non-chain operation a Bluebird because I've so often seen faded billboards on the outskirts of town that say "Eat at the Bluebird—Good Home Cooking."

Bluebirds, happily, are not disappearing from The Road as the Interstates bypass Main Street, but you do have to get off the Interstate to find them. A Bluebird could never, by definition, be located in your Cluster, but when you stop there, ask the gal who pumps your gas or the guy who delivers your pizza where *they* go for breakfast or lunch. That'll be your Bluebird, always downtown on the main drag, or just off on a busy side street.

A Bluebird seldom stands alone, and has no parking lot or drive-up. Look for pickup trucks and overloaded vans with local plates angled in street parking slots with meters ticking. The Bluebird is a store, surrounded by other stores. It is long and narrow, with a counter usually on the right as your enter. The cashier stand is near the door, the cash register atop a beveled glass case displaying candy bars and gum. Tables are center and wooden booths to the left; restrooms are at the back next to the kitchen's swinging doors, *always* labeled "Ladies" and "Gentlemen."

A true Bluebird menu has been *hectographed* the night before, with "today's specials" listed in a wonderful purple ink. (Bluebird proprietors have ignored even mimeograph technology, much less the Xerox or computer printout.) These daily menus, which put to shame the predictable pre-prints of the franchise chains, are then inserted daily behind the isinglass sleeves inside menu folders of red or brown imitation leather with brass corner re-enforcers. You'll know you're in a true Bluebird when you read today's specials: Roast Young Tom Turkey with Giblet Dressing; Chicken-Fried Steak; Pot Roast of Beef; Deep Dish Apple Cobbler. Or check *VEGETABLES: Choose Three.* Don't expect the mundane "tossed-green or Caesar salad, with baked, mashed or fries" of the franchise outfits. A proper Bluebird list will include pickled beets, succotash, sliced tomatoes, corn-on-the-cob, string beans, cottage cheese (okay, it's not a vegetable, but you're expected to know that,) Brussels sprouts, applesauce, okra, potatoes au gratin, candied yams, red cabbage, slaw, and baked beans.

Here are some other traits of the true Bluebird:

1. "Dinner" is at noon.
2. "Pasta" means noodles.
3. Seat yourself. Don't expect Smoking or Non. There's an ashtray on every table.
4. A bell rings when you open the door. A real bell.
5. They always bring you water, but never with ice.
6. No alcohol is served.
7. The homemade soups and pies are *homemade*.
8. The fry cook works the grill in the open, cracks eggs with one hand, and gets off at 11:00 a.m. Bluebirds do not serve breakfast all day.

This is not Fast Food, but a Bluebird waiter or waitress (they still have both) will bring it to you quick and hot, and then might recommend the tapioca pudding for dessert. You should try it.

Signs of the Times

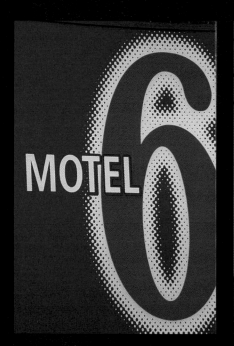

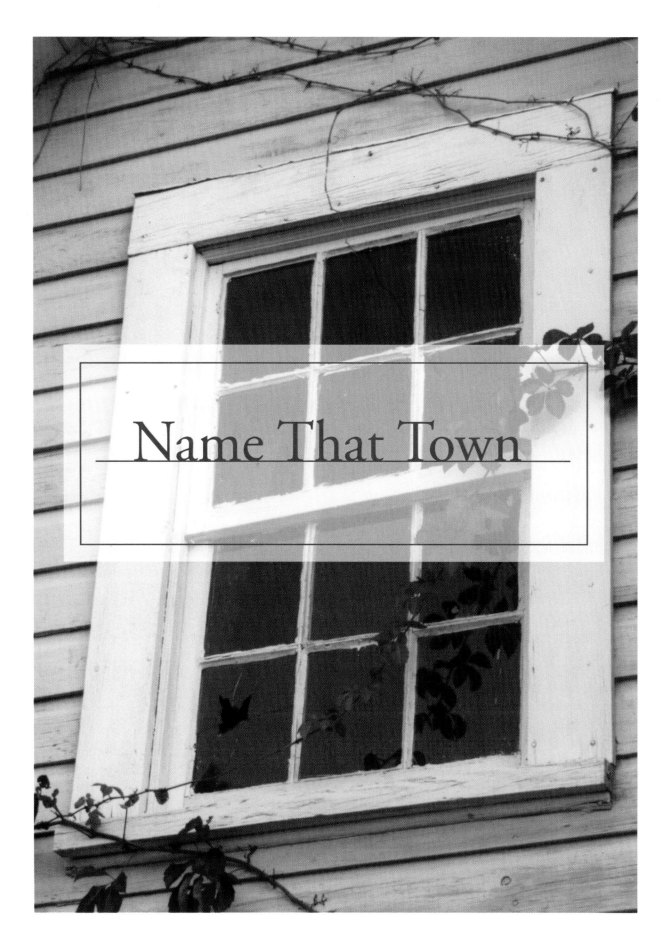

Name That Town

Name that Town

I've loved road maps since I was nine years old

and my mother drove us to California in a 1928 Buick sedan with yellow wooden-spoked wheels and embossed pulldown curtains on the back windows. We took Route 66 and ten days for the trip, and when I wasn't looking out the window or throwing up, I studied our stack of AAA maps (still the best). The names of the towns along the way fascinated me; they were my poetry: Wagon Mound, Winslow, Flagstaff, Barstow. They still are.

Much as I love the offbeat names, I'm comforted too by the familiar ones. Touring the U.S.A. I'm always glad to pull into a Springfield, and I used to be convinced that every state had one. Then I added up all the Greenvilles, and the dozens of Washingtons and Lincolns. These were names of mundane and obvious origin, nowhere near as intriguing as Broken Arrow or Devil's Lake or Biloxi, but I decided recently to test my notion of their ubiquity, and I pass along to you the results of my research.

WASHINGTON is the leader, which seems only right. Twenty-four states have a Washington, thirty-three if you count the counties named for him.

LINCOLN is a close second. Only sixteen cities, but if you add counties, he's up there with the Father of Our Country at thirty-three.

GREENVILLE to my surprise, beats out Springfield by one. You'll find a Greenville in nineteen states, and if you visit towns adorned with other suffixes such as -field, -bush, -wood, -boro, -burg, and -belt, GREEN's in thirty states—almost equal to Washington and Lincoln, and he was never even a president, just a color.

SPRINGFIELD is last but close, and still a major player. Eighteen states claim a Springfield, with more and better suffixes even than Green: -ville, -hill, -vale, -brook, -valley, -town, -hope, and -lake. Counting all these modulations, we get twenty-nine states with a

SPRING of some kind, many in offbeat combinations of great variety, my favorite being Shingle Springs, California.

I have spent many happy hours of travel time speculating how towns with odd names got that way. It's a great road game and I pass it along to you, illustrated by my five theories on: "Why Shingle Springs Did Not Become Just Another Springfield."

I

The town grew around a spring discovered by Mrs. Evian Shingle, a frontier woman who made a small fortune selling tasty fresh water to prospectors, and whose great-granddaughter Evian IV took the company global in 1985.

II

The town was originally just a one-room schoolhouse built near a spring called Dirty Shovel Springs. The teacher, who loved tongue-twisters, put a shingle over the Dirty Shovel sign so she could challenge her students to say "She sells sea shells at the seashore and Shingle Springs."

III

Modern bed springs, invented by C. D. ("Cedar") Shingle (b. 1868) built the Shingle Springs factory there, creating a company town. Shingle, who was single, sold out to Beautyrest in 1927.

IV

The town was originally known as Single Spring (there never was more than one.) It was the site of the area's only saloon until 1885. The clientele, after a few shots of Red Eye, couldn't say "single," and officially renamed the town Shingle Springs, which is the way they'd been pronouncing it all along.

V

The water from the springs flows over a formation of limestone resembling shingles. This explanation is far too logical and was automatically disqualified.

You take it from there.

*The final theme of Scott Joplin's rag
"Elite Syncopations" is not only elite,
but wildly syncopated. It inspired me
to find all these syncopating cities.
You may want to sing along.*

Oklahoma City, Chicago, L.A.,
Tampa, Louisville Kentucky,
Atlanta GA,
Pocatello, San Diego, Tacoma, Duluth,
Cincinnati, Chattanooga, Columbus and Butte.
I hear the rowdy rhythm of the cities and states,
Sacramento California really syncopates,
Altoona Pennsylvania, Miami, Saint Pete,
Complete
The syncopations elite.

Syncopation
How did it get to my feet?
And in this on-time nation
How come everything is off the beat?
Down at a railroad station
Is where I figured it out.
I had a revelation
When I heard the old conductor shout:

Jackson Mississippi, Savannah, Eugene,
Boston, Baltimore, Biloxi,
New Haven, Moline,
Tuscaloosa Alabama, Topeka, Spokane,
Amarillo, Tallahassee, Decatur, Cheyenne.
You'll hear the raggy beat in any city you choose,
Rapid City North Dakota even got the news,
Schenectady New York, and Little Kalamazoo
Will do
The syncopations for you.

Romancing the Malt

Romancing the Malt

Next time you're at a news stand,
ask for the latest issue of "Modern Malt,"

a magazine existing in my imagination. But if enough people ask for it, maybe it will really be out there someday. This nation needs an advocate, an arbiter of that *sine qua non* of the good life, a decent chocolate malted milk, or simply, The Malt.

It's no coincidence that *Modern Malt* and Max Morath share the same initials. The search for the Perfect Malt has been the engine behind my years of life on The Road. Agents, bookers, fans, and friends believe I'm out there for music, money, and immortality. No, I am engaged in an endless quest for The Perfect Malt.

I take the liberty to pass along to you the Ten Principles for the Perfect Malt, as set forth in the *Guide to Malt, (New York. Charles Scribner's Sons. 1928. rev. Larsmont, Inc., 1999)*, in the hope that if you should ever encounter a Malt anywhere in the USA that meets every principle, (a "Ten,") you'll contact me immediately for verification. *Modern Malt*, in turn, will award you with membership in the National Order of Malt, with all the rights and privileges pertaining thereto.

THE TEN PRINCIPLES OF MALT

THE ICE CREAM The Malt must be concocted of real ice cream, with a butter fat content of at least 18 per cent.

THE UTENSILS The ice cream must never be scooped with the fragile spherical blopper used for sundaes and cones, but with the Shovel scoop, the one that looks like it was hand-hammered from cast iron in 1906. The ice cream must be loaded into a large metal can, the Tin, never into a container of styrofoam or paper.

A shocking fault of recent Malt is the increasing use of liquified malt extract, an abomination. The Perfect Malt is made with powdered Malt, plain and unflavored. And don't be bamboozled by "Chocolate-Flavored Malt" powders at the supermarket, dreadful concoctions suitable only in preparing bedtime drinks for infants and insomniacs. The grandeur of Malt—the mystery, actually—is in the intersection of raw Malt flavor, resembling no other, and the familiar sweetness and texture of the ice cream mix.

THE MIXER If you observe that a common kitchen blender is to be used to prepare your

> The search for the Perfect Malt has been the engine behind my years of life on The Road.

THE MILK Whole milk is then added. Never ask for skim. Malting predates the recent wave of aversion to pleasure known as dieting.

THE CONSISTENCY One *drinks* a Malt. It should never be consumed through a straw. The straw is for soda pop and small children, who should be weaned away from it at an early age.

THE CHOCOLATE The ideal Chocolate Malt (is there really any other flavor?) begins, of course, with vanilla ice cream. Plentiful chocolate syrup is then added for flavor, ideally squirted from a permanent fountain container. A seasoned Maltist listens for the squirting sound, the first of several aural rewards of Malting.

> Malting predates the recent wave of aversion to pleasure known as dieting.

Malt, cancel at once. The True Malt is brought to its bubbling best only on a Hamilton Beach unit. Its slender vertical stems, terminating in a mysterious disc the size of a quarter, somehow smoothe and at the same time aerate the Malt. Look for the unique green and chrome exterior of the Hamilton-Beach, the mark of a busy and caring Malt Shoppe.

THE SERVICE The finest Malt, no matter how promising, is a failure if brought to its consumer in the glass only. The Tin, containing additional Malt, must also be brought to the Maltist. Its outer surface should already be sweating from the interface of the cold Malt within and the humidity of the ambient air. Even in arid Colorado this condensation was impressive, and remains a Malt must. Try this test, proven by generations of Malting teenagers: your Malt's condensation should easily support a thumbed inscription of the initials of you and your steady around the outside of the Tin.

THE GLASS The Malt must be presented in a real glass, heavy, flaring from its graceful, beveled base to the smooth circle at its top, where your eager lips will meet your Malt. I once watched a young woman in (name withheld,) Oklahoma, prepare for me what promised to be a Ten, the Perfect Malt. She had it all: rich, thick vanilla ice cream; bountiful chocolate syrup, (I could hear it squirt into the Tin;) a healthy double dollop of classic powdered Malt; just the right amount of whole milk, poured from a quart *bottle*! With a practiced hand she mounted the mixture on a time-worn but immaculate Hamilton-Beach. I turned away, embarrassed by the tenderness I felt developing between us

and my Malt. Moments later I turned back and watched in horror as she poured this treasure into a 12-ounce styrofoam cup and emptied the Tin's remainder into the sink. I wept.

HEARING THE MALT Newcomers to Malt may be unaware of this phenomenon. Raised on the insipid stepchild of Malt known as the "shake," they have never *heard* a Malt. They are accustomed to the boring, soundless flow of the soft ice cream shake into a waxed paper cup, a fast-food ersatz consumed by rote and without passion. The Perfect Malt sings "bah-LUMP, bah-LUMP" to you, as the still-lumpy mixture first descends into the glass. Here the art of the Malt Maker meets its ultimate test. The Tin must be removed from the Hamilton-Beach at just the right moment. Liquefaction has taken place, but a few strategic blobs of ice cream must remain to produce the perfect "bah-LUMP."

LOOKING AHEAD Is there hope for a Malt Renaissance? Time will tell. Meanwhile my own search for a Ten, a Perfect Malt, goes on. Not long ago I was served a decent 8.0 Malt in a candy-striped Arizona emporium called Toot's Sweets, prepared by a bright teenager who followed my modest suggestions. And I realized that if the malt is to reclaim its vaunted position in American life, it will be up to the young people of the nation to reeducate their Boomer parents, who were brain-washed into the belief that the tasteless "shake" of late Twentieth-Century America in any way equals the splendor of the True Malt. It is with these daring youngsters, who, after all, have recently embraced swing dancing and a clean shave, that the future of Malt must be entrusted.

Loving the Ragtime Life

Loving the Ragtime Life

Ragtime:

a written form of piano music in duple time that surfaced in America around 1900, resembling the march in pattern, and juxtaposing syncopated figures in the right hand against steady rhythm in the left.

Is that the same thing these two young guys are singing about in 1900?

"Got ragtime habits and I talk that way,
Sleep in ragtime and I rag all day..."

"Living a Ragtime Life"
Gene Jefferson and Bob Roberts, 1900

Sounds like we're talking about two different kinds of music here, like Gene and Bob were possessed by a force of nature. The cool definition of ragtime (above) may mollify the musicologists, but ragtime isn't at all cool, it's hot. It TAKES OVER. I know, because it happened to me too, about forty years after it clobbered Gene and Bob. I caught ragtime like you catch the flu, and I never got over it.

It has taken me, as you can see, into ancient municipal auditoriums and slick new performing arts centers all over the country, presenting my ragtime obsession on stage. I work backstage with helpful high school kids and grizzled union pros who are ragtime neutral, but to whom I owe a continual tip of the hat. Their next assignment could be a rock concert or Shakespeare, but they serve every performance in ways the audience never sees or thinks about.

Every so often I rename these shows I take on the road, but "ragtime" is always in the title, and I'm continually amazed at how thoroughly that mild case of ragtime flu in childhood came to infect my adult life and livelihood. It took me a while to diagnose this ragtime affliction, and the closer I got to it the more elusive it became. Happily I quit fretting somewhere along the line, having realized that everything about music is a mystery anyway, and since ragtime is just that—music—elusive it may remain.

Anyway, as a teenager I was listening mostly to jazz, not ragtime, and trying to play the piano like Teddy Wilson. And if I wasn't singing in the Glee Club or the church choir I was forming a barbershop quartet. Music was fun. The serious Max in those days was a physics and math maven who dreamed of time travel and rocket science. Here I was, assuring cynical pals guzzling chocolate malts at Murray's Drugstore in Colorado Springs that we'd land on the moon before the year 2000, little dreaming that the moon in my future would be, rather, the one that rhymed with June, tune, and that sneaky euphemism from the Good Old Days, "spoon," with its randy implications. My interest in science, by the way, has remained, but my idols

> I caught ragtime like you catch the flu, and I never got over it.

later in life would not be Bill Gates and Captain Kirk, but Thomas Edison and the Wright Brothers.

It wasn't the first time the math/science bug and the music bug had bitten the same guy at the same time. They say it's a common affinity. I was learning the periodic table one week and *Humoresque* the next, studying spherical trig at school and counterpoint after school. But ragtime? Not yet, though my mother often punched it out on the Sohmer Upright in our parlor on East Del Norte Street. She'd pop open the piano bench and pull out *Raggin' the Scale or Dill Pickles*, and the neighbors would come by with casseroles and home brew. But Colorado Springs was certainly no ragtime hothouse during my 1930s and '40s coming-of-age. So how come my mother had all those rags in our piano bench?

Gladys Ramsell Morath was born and raised in the southeastern Iowa town of Ottumwa—a town close enough to the ragtime mecca of St.

but he couldn't read music. It was a ragtime symbiosis. Young barrister Richard Ramsell brought home the sheet music for the latest ragtime hit so his kid sister could play it for him. Two or three passes by Gladys and he'd own it by ear, in his style and in his key. (Ear players usually favor the key of C, mostly white keys, or F#, mostly black.) I have no idea what Uncle Dick's home key was, but when he played the rags they say he did them slow and dreamy, and in a rhythm like no one else.

> It took me a while to diagnose this ragtime affliction, and the closer I got to it the more elusive it became.

Gladys Ramsell, meanwhile, imprinted the rags in her memory and her fingers and a few years later hauled that sheet music west when she moved to Colorado Springs around 1919 to play for the silent pictures at the Princess Theater. My father, Fred Morath, was assistant manager (read night projectionist,) and the rest is history. Mine. Not, but the way, to suggest that I underwent prenatal ragtime influence because of all this. I doubt that my mother played much ragtime for the movies, except perhaps the redoubtable *Maple Leaf*, opting instead to match the changing moods of the two-reelers by cobbling together *Poet and Peasant*, *The Midnight Fire Alarm*, and *Hearts and Flowers*, sight-reading as always from piles

Louis that the syncopations and the sheet music could drift easily that far north. My mother was next-to-youngest in a multi-kid family still living on a ten-acre farm, but wishing they weren't and soon enough gone. The eldest of the brood was my Uncle Dick, the family artist, lawyer, and alcoholic. He also, I was told, played great ragtime piano, but only by ear. I saw him just once, when I was nine years old, and must have heard him play. But all I can remember was watching in fascination as my uncle filled a huge glass with beer, dropped in a raw egg and two shots of Old Crow, and downed it all in one draft.

My mother, like most girls in those days, "took piano," and by age ten or so she could deliver a clean-cut sight read of most anything put in front of her. But she couldn't improvise. Big brother Dick could play anything he heard,

Sohmer in the parlor. She hadn't lost her touch.

The first rag she urged me to try was Scott Joplin's *Original Rags*, his first published rag, released a few months before the *Maple Leaf* in 1899 and apparently quite popular, though overshadowed later by the barn-burning *Maple Leaf*. Copies of *Original* aren't all that rare, and there it was in our piano bench. I took it on around age ten, I think, finding it not as hard to play as *Maple Leaf*, or Confrey's *Kitten on the Keys* and Felix Arndt's *Nola*, also napping in the bench. It fit young hands and was in "easy" keys. It had five themes, but you could skip the intimidating theme IV and proceed to V, with its aching parallel thirds and intoxicating syncopations, which beg you, subtlely, to add even more. Joplin, by the way, had often used the word "intoxicating" to describe the effects of ragtime, and I don't know of a better one except maybe "rush." Ragtime's magic brew of sweet melody, chromatic harmony, and impelling syncopation does indeed bypass the intellect and go directly into the bloodstream.

of sheet music on the Princess Theater's baby grand. It was only after marrying the erstwhile projectionist, moving on to her first jobs in advertising and journalism, and birthing two boys, my brother Fred and me, that she finally found time at home to revisit the rags on the

There are only two kinds of music, said the masterful Eubie Blake. Good and bad.

Happily I quit fretting somewhere along the line, having realized that everything about music is a mystery anyway . . .

I then began my conquest of the *Maple Leaf Rag*, but it took me two years before I had the courage to play it for my pals. And meanwhile another rich vein had turned up in the piano bench—a handsome John Stark & Sons folio with a dozen other great Missouri ragtime secrets. Joplin's ingratiating *Easy Winners* was in there, and the Joplin-Hayden collaboration *Sunflower Slow Drag*. I discovered James Scott's *Hilarity Rag* with its crunchy, full-throated octaves in the syncopated right hand. Hard! You learned a few measures at a time and studied how these masters turned around a repeat or laid down a four-bar intro. It was all a big adventure, a treasure hunt.

So ragtime was around when I was a kid, but it wasn't *mine* yet. In junior high school I dreamed of jazz. I discovered Fats Waller. I still have a 78-rpm record of his "Handful of Keys." I couldn't play even the watered-down arrangements of his stuff that you could buy at Miller's Music Store, but I could sure try. Then I found Tatum. I do believe that pianists of any age or persuasion will agree that on first hearing Art Tatum, we all decide to quit piano and take up kazoo. But we don't. We invite Tatum into our subconscious, as I did, with his majestic technique and transcendent ideas and tap into him for the rest of our lives.

I began to store other players in my improvisational chops: Frankie Carle, Earl Hines, Eddy Duchin. In high school I unearthed Billy Kyle and Jess Stacy; then as a college freshman working as a part-time announcer at a radio station, I was surrounded by hundreds of records and 16-inch "electrical transcriptions." Nat Cole and Mary Lou Williams and Eddie

Heywood entered my life. I found myself playing pretty good jazz, improvising in any key (well, not great in E and B,) and my phone started to ring, older guys with pickup bands calling. "Can you play with a band at the Acacia Hotel Saturday? Lion's Club Dinner Dance, Nine to One, twenty bucks?"

"*Yes!*"

By now I knew most of the standard dance tunes in the standard keys, and had joined the Musician's Union. I was seventeen, I was happy, and I didn't even have a girl friend.

How did this lead to a lifelong devotion to ragtime? Tell you what. I don't think music fits cozy pigeon-holes. Sure, "ragtime" brought deepening syncopation into American music, and that breakthrough has driven our music throughout the century. But what's in a name? Was Art Tatum playing ragtime? Did it guide George Gershwin's mind and fingers? Was Errol Garner a ragtime man?

Who cares? I wanted to own them all.

And I didn't trust all those labels anyway—ragtime, jazz, folk, rock, and swing. They don't mean very much musically. They're trade terms made up for the convenience of people who sort CD's at Tower Records or write articles for trade papers.

There are only two kinds of music, said the masterful Eubie Blake. Good and bad.

I think I saw, too, that ragtime was simply part of the whole. It was music. Its left hand was not that dissimilar to Chopin's in the "Minute Waltz" (I made it once in 2:06). Its harmonies were in the Broadway ball park. I liked that. I didn't want to separate music. I still don't. I'm afraid if I have to stick labels on it I'll have to choose up sides.

I never met Irving Berlin personally but was honored with a phone call every so often. And he advised me to beware of those labels because they contained no precise musical meaning. The only one that did, he said, was the blues, not because of its lyrical content, but because of its precise chord sequence, known to musicians and singers of every stripe in every language. It's a 12-measure schematic of the I, IV, and V chords in a prescribed order. Sure, you can flat or sharp any interval inside those chords, but depart from the

sequence and you're playing something else, not the blues.

I recalled those club dates with pickup jazz groups that I began as a seventeen-year-old in a cold sweat. The leader usually said let's get acquainted and play some blues in G or Bb or whatever, and off we'd go, young Max getting loose because he had learned that on the fifth measure you went to the IV^7 chord.

And ragtime? It hooked me first and for a long time as a neat niche in the big world of music. Thanks to Gladys Ramsell Morath and her magic piano bench, I had stored the ragtime reach into my childhood chops. So later, when the dormant history buff in my cluttered persona finally surfaced and I fell for the turn-of-the-century era that spawned ragtime, I could meld music with manners and morals as I dug

in that particular trove of American treasure. I've always found ragtime to be as elusive as ever, a mood more than just a kind of music, which speaks to us about our national gifts and our sins, which ignited the fire that became American Pop, and leaves us, still intoxicated, in mystery.

Community Concerts

"I love a **piano**, I love a **piano**,
I **love** to hear somebody **play**. . ."

"...so you can **keep** your
fiddle and your **bow**,
give **me** a P-I-A-N-O-O-O. . ."

"I love to watch someone run their
fingers o'er the keys,
the ivories. . ."

"...got a ragtime **piano**
in my **ragtime** flat. . ."

"Drinkin' **ragtime** coffee from a **ragtime** cup,

Gonna **keep** raggin', til I **can't** stand up...."

Somehow ragtime gets you goin'
From your hat down to your shoes

Maple Leaf Rag, I need you like a daddy
Needs his momma
when he's got the blues.

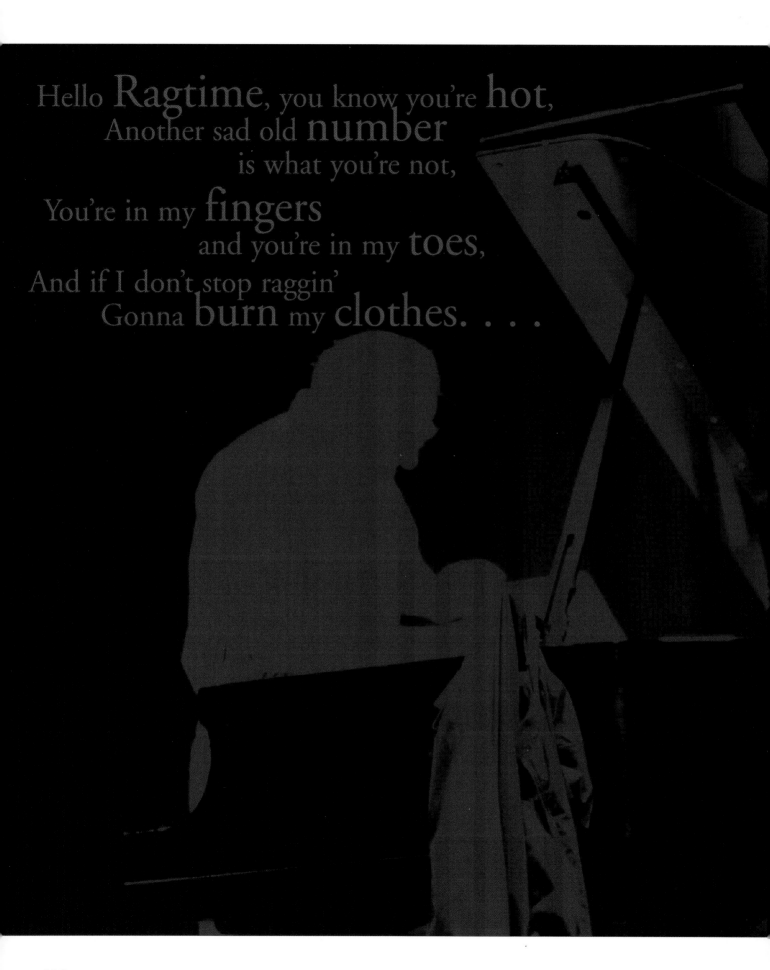

Hello Ragtime, you know you're hot,
Another sad old number
is what you're not,
You're in my fingers
and you're in my toes,
And if I don't stop raggin'
Gonna burn my clothes. . . .

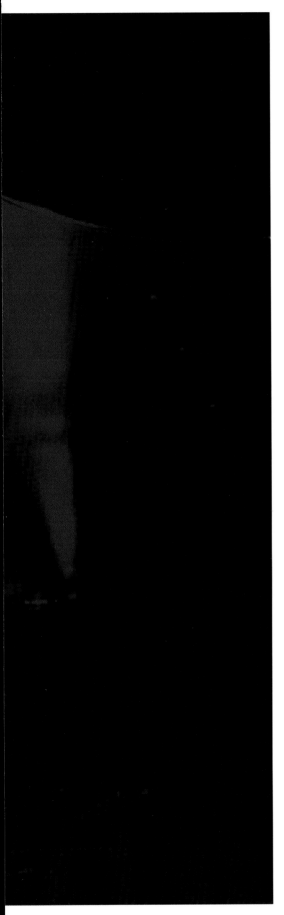

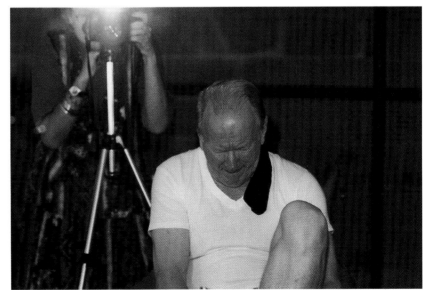

River Road

River Road

It's a great big, all-out, no doubt blowout
Party on the river Queens.
Better grab your honey, bring along your money
For the whisky and rice and beans.

If you can't stand lookin' at Creole cookin'
Go back to your northern scenes,
'Cause you're gonna be jazzin' and razz-z-ma-tazzin'
In the city of New Orleans!

Somehow ragtime keeps you goin'
'Til the break of day,
And on the show boat it's here to stay,
The river rolls in a diff'rent way . . .

Saint Louie's jumpin' in ragtime rhythm,
Memphis is hummin' the blues right with 'em,
Upstream 'n down, most ev'ry town
Rattles and revels in music the devil's in,
You'd have to be deaf, or as mean as Satan,
Not to be jazzin' and syncopatin'
Most ev'ry night it's a wonderful sight,
At a Mississippi cabaret.

Northern Exposure

This photograph suits me just fine. I prefer to record the scene rather than to play a role in it and my father, who was an engineer by day and photographer by night, is to blame. E. T. Skomars' darkroom was the perfect escape in my childhood. It held great mystery—the glow of the red lamp, the smell of the mixed chemicals in pans placed side by side and the magic of paper changing into images before my very eyes. In the early years I was his favorite model for his Speed Graphic camera—that is until I could hold a camera myself. From that moment on I preferred to be behind the lens instead of in front of it.

Whether on the road recording Max's life or in my New York portrait studio, I bring inherited respect for the visual. With a photographer father and an artist mother I was encouraged to spot "the beautiful" in each creature and every soul. I've spent over thirty years of professional experience in public relations for educational institutions of all sizes. But it is my love of photographing the unique and my passion for travel that have allowed me to visit and record the people and sights in over fifty-five countries.

As I witness the shifting northern light in my studio, I am mindful of the ongoing lessons photography has taught me. They're not about shutter speed and focal length. Rather they are about people. Most people don't like to be photographed and I understand why. The studio is quiet and it's just us and the camera. And the camera does not lie.

When I light your face, focus the lens, and snap the shutter, I see your essence, your kindness, your humor. It's all there. I don't need special effects—just your honesty and a little luck.

That's why I love photography. It is both a skill and an art, and it is by nature a very private business.

Here's looking at you.

Diane Fay Skomars

A Day in the Life

A Day in the Life

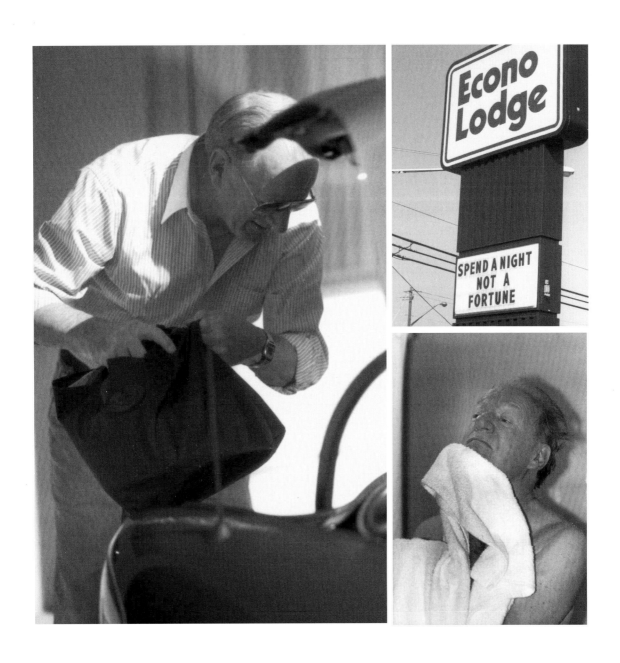

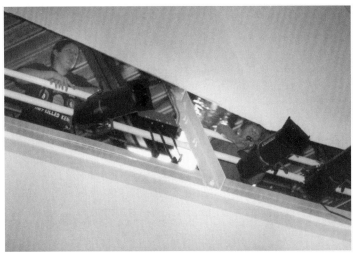

NO SMOKING ON STAGE

Thinking About the Music

Thinking About the Music

George M. Cohan, the "Yankee Doodle Boy," once said there wouldn't be any American music without the Jews, the Irish, and the Negroes.

I don't think George M. believed these three ethnic or racial groups were intrinsically more talented than others. Stephen Foster was none of the above, nor was John Philip Sousa. Cohan meant that the door into the world of popular music and theater and vaudeville was one of the first to open for the newcomer—meaning generally the persecuted and the reviled. Other doors were still closed.

But social critics and musicologists ought someday soon to give up tracking race and ethnicity in every note of American music. The music itself has no language or nationality. It's "American" if it happened in America. Much of it was indeed created by gifted people who, as Cohan understood, were doing their work under the imperative of economic survival, and in a more congenial world might have entered the doors to law or medicine or business. But their hard times were to shape a rich cultural legacy for us all.

Talent, with irresistible momentum, flows impartially through every new generation. In youth it is exuberant, and if hobbled by adversity, all the more insistent and overpowering. Gifted young black men, after the war between the states, sat down at the pianos of America and brought a portion of their African heritage—the

Eubie Blake
and Noble Sissle

play the pump organ at church when you were four years old, you took your nickname "Eubie" and wore it through a life in music that lasted one hundred years and in its final days was honored by an entire nation and its president.

If your folks were Russian Jews fleeing the pogroms and you ended up broke on the Lower East Side of New York, and saw there was money to be made in this new game called "popular music," and you had tunes and rhymes ringing in your head, you opened a little publishing company, changed your name to Irving Berlin, and gave us songs to sing for almost a century.

profound ability to subdivide the beat—to that most European of musical instruments. Sifting Baptist hymns and Irish jigs and British marches through piano hands of awesome agility they created a new musical synthesis that took first the odd name "ragtime," and as it matured in the full family of instruments, the equally beguiling "jazz."

Would it have happened without them? Clearly not, by its very definition and nature. Could it have happened anywhere else but America? Absolutely not. Talent and heritage meshed with ambition and merchandising, and off we went into a new century with what came to be known as American Popular Music.

If your parents had left behind a life of slavery and moved to Baltimore to seek a new life, and if you, James Hubert Blake, their only surviving son, found you could

George M. Cohan.

and Hart, Harold Arlen—what a blessing that their forebears walked away from the cruel persecutions of Europe, so that their talented, hungry offspring could create the great body of work that is the American musical. Do I, a WASP from the West, own them and their music? Absolutely.

Was ragtime "black?" Wrong question. Were its first great figures black? Of course. Does that mean because I'm "white" I have no equity in that music, that I don't understand it? Ridiculous. I was once scolded by a talk show host who said I had "no right" as a white person to interpret Scott Joplin, a black. I recovered just enough to ask him (he was white) whether it was okay for Joplin, because he wasn't Polish, to play Chopin.

And if, a generation or two earlier, your folks got the hell out of Ireland because they were starving to death, and found themselves in the Land of the Free, clinging to the bottom rung of its society, and you heard that a fellow named Harrigan and some others amongst your landsmen were making good money in the show business, you changed the spelling of your name from Keohan to Cohan so agents could pronounce it, formed the Four Cohans and hit the circuit, passing the passion and the hunger on to your son George M.

And jazz? Checking its acknowledged originators from King Oliver and Louis Armstrong, through Fletcher Henderson and Duke Ellington to Count Basie and Oscar Peterson, black, no question. Have I a claim to their music? Of course. Has it inspired me? All my life. The only colors on the printed pages of music have always been black and white.

Others pushed through the same door and entered the palmy business of music and entertainment—thousands of remarkably talented American men and women of hyphenated origin, many of whom, given the choice or the chance, would have become doctors or diplomats, teachers or heads of corporations. But here first was a ticket to self-esteem and survival, and to a livelihood. Entering in greater and greater numbers, they enriched a century of American music.

Is our musical theater "Jewish?" Yes, thank God. Kern and Gershwin, Berlin and Rodgers

Irving Berlin

The Recordings

We probably should call this a "discography," but since it also includes a video and some piano rolls, "recordings" seems to cover the ground better. This is not a complete list. There are reissues and overseas licensing deals that are impossible to track. But most of the recordings since the first one in 1954 are listed, with time and place, and the names of personnel involved.

—Max Morath

1954 Max Morath plays at the Gold Bar Room (Piano/Vocal)
Gold Camp Recordings (No #); 10" Mono LP on green vinyl
Recorded at KCMS radio studios, Manitou Springs, Colorado
Producers: Max Morath & C.M. "Bud" Edmonds
Engineer: Bud Edmonds
Drums: George Marvin
Cover Art: Herman Raymond
Notes: Marshall Sprague

1956 Max Morath plays at the Gold Bar Room (Piano/Vocal)
Gold Camp Recordings (No #); 10" Mono LP on gold vinyl
(Four sides also released on 45-rpm EP, gold vinyl)
Recorded on the Peerless Orchestrion at "Ghost Town," Colorado City, Colorado
Producers: Max Morath & C. M. "Bud" Edmonds
Engineer: Bud Edmonds
Cover Art: Herman Raymond
Notes: Marshall Sprague

This album is actually volume II of "Max Morath at the Gold Bar Room," but is not so-labeled. Musical repertory is entirely different from Volume I. The cover painting by Herman Raymond is rendered without change but in different colors. Sprague's notes are identical.

1957 Max Morath at The Mighty Gold Bar Piano (Piano/Vocal)
Gold Camp Recordings (KCMS 1129-30); 12" Mono LP on gold vinyl
Recorded on the Peerless Orchestrion at "Ghost Town," Colorado City, Colorado
Producers: Max Morath & C. M. "Bud" Edmonds
Engineer: Bud Edmonds
Cover Art: Don Willis
Notes: Marshall Sprague

Music for Moochers, Gold Diggers and Cattle Rustlers (Piano)
Talking Machine Records, a product of San Francisco Record Corp. (TM-4); 12" Mono LP
This recording contains material from the 1956 and 1957 Gold Camp Recordings, piano only; voices and sound effects added by SFRC.
Recorded on the Peerless Orchestrion at "Ghost Town," Colorado City, Colorado
Producers: Max Morath, C. M. "Bud" Edmonds, and Al Levitt
Engineer: Bud Edmonds
Cover Art: (new) Don Willis
Notes: Marshall Sprague & Al Levitt

This album was re-issued in 1960 in Mono and Stereo 12" LP by Barbary Coast Records (BC 33004) San Francisco. Same cover, contents, and notes.)

1958 Honky-Tonk in Hi-fi (Piano/Vocal)
Gold Camp Recordings (No #); 12" Mono LP
Producers: Max Morath, C. M. "Bud" Edmonds
Engineer: Bud Edmonds
Cover Art: Don Willis

1959 More Morath (Piano/Vocal)
Gold Camp Recordings (KCMS 1168-69); 12" Mono LP
Recorded Candlelight Inn, Colorado Springs
Producers: Max Morath & C. M. "Bud" Edmonds
Engineer: Bud Edmonds
Cover Photo: Bud Edmonds
Design: Don Willis
Notes: Max Morath

1963 Unreleased Singles: Epic (79276-77)
Vocals with Piano & Orchestra: "Oh, Mister Johnson (Turn Me Loose)" and "The Blues I've Got"
Recorded at Columbia Records 30th Street Studio, New York
Arranged and conducted by Stan Applebaum
Vocal back-up group: The Free Wheelers
Producer: Bob Morgan

Presenting That Celebrated Maestro Max Morath...(Piano/Vocal)
Epic (24006) 12" LP Mono & Stereo
Recorded before a live audience, Columbia Records 30th Street Studio, New York
Producer: Bob Morgan
Cover Photo: Bob Cato
Notes: Max Morath

1964 Oh, Play That Thing! The Ragtime Era
Epic (24106) 12" LP Mono & Stereo
Piano and vocals with studio ensemble: bass, drums, guitar, banjo
Recorded at Columbia Records Nashville Studios
Vocal Accompaniment: The Jordanaires
Producer: Bob Morgan
Cover Photo: Henry Parker

Unreleased Album: Max Morath's Original Rag Quartet
Epic (92730-40)
Vocal & instrumental: with Jim Tyler, banjo; Barry Kornfeld, guitar & 5-string banjo; Felix Pappalardi, guitarron
Recorded at Columbia Records 30th Street Studio, New York; Fall, 1964
Producer: Bob Morgan

This is the quartet personnel of the Original Rag Quartet as it played New York's Village Vanguard the summer of 1964 and later performed in concerts nationally, and with Dinah Shore in Las Vegas and elsewhere. Two selections from the album were released for promotion only on 45-rpm singles: "My Gal is a Highborn Lady," and "Dill Pickles."

1966 They All Play Ragtime (Piano Solos)
Jazzology Jazz Piano Heritage Series, Vol. II (JCE-52); 12" Mono LP
With other artists: Tom Shea, John Arpin, Trebor Tichenor, Donald Ashwander, and Peter Lundberg
Producers: Samuel Charters & Rudi Blesh
Notes: Rudi Blesh

1968 The Entertainer and Other Rag Classics (Piano/Quartet)
Arpeggio (1204); 12" Mono and Stereo LP
Featuring: Jim Tyler, tenor and 5-string banjo; Al Harris, guitar; and Bill Turner, bass
Recorded at Hallmark Studios, Toronto
Arrangements by Max Morath; additional arranging by Jim Tyler and Fred Karlin
Producer: John Arpin
Engineer: Mel Crosby
Cover photo/design: Baron McCormick and Anne Arpin
Notes: Rudi Blesh

This album (recorded in the fall of 1967, released in 1968) recreates in new recordings much of the material first arranged for the Original Rag Quartet, but never released by Columbia Records Epic label (above), plus additional material arranged for the session. Selections are instrumental only, except for one group vocal.

1969 Max Morath at the Turn of the Century (Piano/Vocals with orchestra)
RCA Victor (LSO-1159); Original Cast Recording Series; 12" Stereo LP
Arranged and conducted by Fred Karlin; additional arrangements by Ray Wright
Recorded at RCA Studio B, New York
Producer: Andy Wiswell
Engineer: Ernie Oelrich
Notes: Max Morath

All the songs and rags on this album were included in the Off-Broadway show "Max Morath at the Turn of the Century," Jan Hus Theater, New York, February-June, 1969. (Orchestra arrangements added for the recording only.)

1972 The Best of Scott Joplin and Other Rag Classics (Piano w/ quartet)
Vanguard Recording Society, Inc. (VSD 39-40); Double album, Stereo LP's, ("also playable Mono")
Sides I & II VSD 40 are remastered from Arpeggio 1204 (above) with minor edits.
Sides I & II VSD 39 are newly-recorded piano solos
Recorded at Vanguard West 23rd Street Studio, New York
Producer: Jack Lothrop
Engineer: Jeff Zaraya
Cover Art: Eric von Schmidt
Notes: Rudi Blesh

This piano disc in this set was reissued on Vanguard Mid-Line Series (VMS-73106) single LP as "Max Morath Plays the Best of Scott Joplin and Other Rag Classics," 1984; cover design Greco/Emmi Inc., after von Schmidt; Notes: Nancy Toff
NOTE: All subsequent Vanguard releases were recorded at Vanguard's West 23rd Street Studio, New York, unless otherwise indicated.

1973 The World of Scott Joplin (Piano Solos)
Vanguard (310); Everyman Series, Stereo LP (also VSQ 30031 Quad)
Producer: Jack Lothrop
Cover Art: Eric von Schmidt
Notes: Max Morath

1974 Irving Berlin—The Ragtime Years (Vocal with Orchestra)
Vanguard (79346); Stereo LP; Quad 40042
Arranged and conducted by Manny Albam
Producer: Seymour Solomon
Cover: Design, Jues Halfant, from a slide from the collection of John W. Ripley
Notes: Robert Kimball

1975 Ragtime Special (Piano with various bands, ensembles)
RCA Camden (ADL2-0778); double stereo LP's
Remastered reissue: four selections from "Max Morath at the Turn of the Century" (1969)
Other artists: Muggsy Spanier, Poppa John Gordy, Del Wood, "The Ragtimers"
Producer: Ethel Gabriel
Remaster engineer: Bernard Keville

The World of Scott Joplin, Vol. 2 (Piano Solos)
Vanguard (351); Everyman Series, stereo LP
Producer: Jeff Zaraya
Notes: Lois Gertman

Music at the Turn of the Century (Double Stereo LP)
Distributed by American Heritage; CBS Columbia Records
Special Products (LOC #75-750041); reissues of several selections from previously issued Epic Recordings (above;) with other artists including Mitch Miller, Eubie Blake, Andre Kostelanetz, Wally Rose. (Note: "Scott Joplin's New Rag" credited to me is actually Wally Rose at the piano.)

1976 Max Morath Plays Ragtime (Piano Solos)
Vanguard (VSD 83-84); "Twofer" reissue of "The World of Scott Joplin" (Vols. 1 & 2)
Producers: Jack Lothrop and Jeff Zaraya
Cover Art: Eric von Schmidt (new)
Notes: Lois Gertman

Jonah Man (and other songs of the Bert Williams Era) (Vocals with Piano and Ensemble)
Vanguard (79378); Stereo LP
Ensemble arrangements by Max Morath for guitar, banjo, harmonica, bass, drums
Producer: Jeff Zaraya
Engineer: John Kilgore
Cover Photo: Joel Brodsky/Frank Kolleogy

Good Friends are for Keeps (Vocals with Orchestra; other artists)
12" LP produced by the Bell Telephone System in celebration of the 100th anniversary of the invention of the telephone (1876); not for sale.
Period songs about the telephone arranged and conducted by Manny Albam; other artist's reissues include Glenn Miller, Vicki Carr, The Fifth Dimension, Glen Campbell
Producers: Manny Albam, Max Morath
Cover Photographs: Slides from the collection of John W. Ripley
Notes: Max Morath

1977 The Ragtime Women (Piano with Quintet)
Vanguard (79402); Stereo LP
Quintet arrangements by Max Morath for guitar,
banjo/mandolin, cello, bass
Producers: Robert G. Lurie & Max Morath
Engineers: Charlie Repka, Jeff Zaraya
Cover Art: Thomas Digrazia
Notes: Max Morath

These Charming People (Vocals with Piano)
RCA Red Seal (ARL1-2491); Stereo LP; also available
on "Stereo 8" and cassette with Joan Morris, soprano;
William Bolcom, piano
Duets by the Gershwins, Jerome Kern, Rodgers & Hart
Recorded at RCA Studio B, New York
Producer: Sam Parkins
Engineers: Anthony Salvatore, Paul Goodman,
James Crotty
Cover: Design J. J. Stelmach; Photography David
B. Hecht
Notes: Robert Kimball

**Living A Ragtime Life [A One-Man Show by Max
Morath] (Piano/Vocal)**
Vanguard (79391); Stereo LP
"Recorded in live performance at Vanguard's 23rd
Street Studio . . ."
Producer: Seymour Solomon
Engineers: Charlie Repka, Mark Berry, Jeff Zaraya
Cover Photo: Frank Kolleogy
Notes: Robert Kimball

**1978 Don't Give The Name a Bad Place (Vocal with
Quartet, other artists)**
New World Records (NW 265); Stereo LP, in New
World's Recorded Anthology of American Music
Max Morath sings the songs of Harrigan & Hart
Piano & Conductor: Dick Hyman
Other Soloists: Danny Barker, Clifford Jackson
Recorded at Columbia Recording Studios, 30th Street,
New York
Producer: Sam Parkins
Engineers: Stan Tonkel, Russ Payne, Don Van
Gordon
Cover Art: Charles Witham, courtesy of Museum of
the City of New York; design, Elaine
Sherer Cox
Notes: Richard M. Sudhalter

**1979 Max Morath in Jazz Country (Vocal/Piano with
Band)**
Vanguard (79418); Stereo LP
Band arrangements by Richard Sudhalter, Manny
Albam, Max Morath
Featuring Richard Sudhalter, cornet & flugelhorn
Producer: Pete Spargo
Engineer: Jeff Zaraya
Cover Photo: Frank Kolleogy
Notes: Dan Langan

The Great American Piano Bench (Piano Solos)
"A Turn-of-the-Century Keyboard Sampler"
Vanguard (79429); Stereo LP
Producer: Max Morath
Engineer: Fred Miller
Cover Art: Eric von Schmidt; design, Jules Halfant
Notes: Max Morath

1981 More Rodgers and Hart (Vocal Duets with Piano)
RCA Red Seal (ARL1 4676); Stereo LP
Max Morath "Guest Artist" with Joan Morris, soprano,
and William Bolcom, piano
Recorded at RCA Studio A, New York
Producer: Leroy Parkins
Engineers: Paul Goodman, Johnnie Cue
Cover: J. J. Stelmach, Gary Kelley, Nick
Sangiamo
Notes: Robert Kimball

**Max Morath and His Ragtime Stompers (Piano with
Ensemble)**
Vanguard (79440); Stereo LP
Arrangements by Max Morath, with improvisation by
studio ensemble, featuring Bill Keith, banjo; Eric
Weissberg, guitar; Ken Kosek, fiddle; others
Producer: Maynard Solomon
Engineer: Tom Lazarus
Cover: Don Lewis

1984 Pop Goes the Music—The Max Morath Quintet
Normacks (No #); cassette only; Normacks (as #100)
issued on ESI (206), Stereo LP. (Columbia Artists cus
tom label); selections are from "Pop Goes the Music:
American Popular Music...and How It Got That Way";
concert vehicle on national tours for Columbia Artists,
1984–1987. Quintet arrangements by Max Morath and
Jim McElwaine
Recorded at Vanguard Studios, 23rd Street, New York
Producer: Max Morath
Engineer: Jeff Zaraya
Notes: Max Morath

**1986 Cripple Creek—A Ragtime Suite for Piano (Piano
Solos)**
Mel Bay Publications (94094C); cassette only
Piano compositions of Max Morath; issued on cassette
with print folio of the music
Recorded at Seltzer Sound Studio, New York
Producers: Max Morath and William Bay
Engineer: Carl Seltzer

1987 Best of Ragtime Piano (Piano Solos)
Mel Bay Publications (94180C); cassette only
Twelve classic piano rags issued on cassette with print
folio of the music
Recorded at Seltzer Sound Studio, New York
Producers: Max Morath and William Bay
Engineer: Carl Seltzer

Living a Ragtime Life (Piano/Vocal)
Normacks Inc. (NX101); cassette only
Recorded at Music Division Studios, SUNY Purchase,
New York
Producers: Max Morath & Jim McElwaine
Engineers: Jim McElwaine and Dan Berlinger
Cover Art: Al Hirschfeld, from caricature commis-
sioned 1969
Notes: Max Morath

*This recording is not a reissue of "Living a Ragtime Life"
(Vanguard 79391,) although it contains a few of the same selections. The 1987 version was recorded after the Off-Broadway run
of "Living a Ragtime Life," November-December, 1986, in prepa-
ration for national tour; it contains most of the music from my
one-man show at that time, and under that name. The Compact
Disc of similar name appears in 1989.*

In 1987 the Welk Music Group, which had acquired the Vanguard catalog, began reissuing on Compact Disc (CD) and cassette (CS) many of the Vanguard LP's listed above. Contents and credits remain the same unless otherwise noted. All these analog LP's were, of course, digitally remastered. Reissues retain the Vanguard label, as a Welk Record Group Company.

1987 REISSUES

The Best of Scott Joplin and other Rag Classics
Vanguard-Welk (39/40); CD & CS
Data as above
Two selections deleted from LP set: "Original Rags" and "Slippery Elm"

The World of Scott Joplin
Vanguard-Welk (310); CD & CS
Data as above

The World of Scott Joplin (Vol. 2)
Vanguard-Welk (351); CD & CS
Data as above

1989 Max Morath—Living a Ragtime Life (Piano/Vocal)
SoloArt, a label of Jazzology/GHB, New Orleans (SACD-110); Compact Disc only
Additional material added to Normacks 101 cassette (above) recorded at Seltzer Sound, New York
Producer: Max Morath, George Buck
Production Coordinator: Jon P. Pult
Engineer: Carl Seltzer
Cover Art: Al Hirschfeld

1990 Fountain Favorites (with other artists; Vocals with Orchestra)
Custom (cassette only) recording produced by the Coca-Cola Company to mark their 100th year in business. All the songs are about Coca-Cola. With Joan Morris, soprano, and William Bolcom, pianist, Barbara Riffe, Dalia Silve
Orchestra conducted by Manny Albam
Arrangements: Manny Albam, William Bolcom, Max Morath, Yomo Toro
Recorded at RCA Studio A, New York
Executive Producer: Barbara Charles
Producer: Leroy Parkins
Artistic Director: Max Morath
Engineers: Paul Goodman, James Nichols
Advisor & Editing Engineer: Michael Lorimer
Re-mix Engineer: Jeff Zaraya
Design: Staples & Charles Ltd.

The Ragtime Century (Piano Solos)
PianoMania (103); CD only
Originally recorded on Yamaha C7F piano with Yamaha digital Disklavier system; CD from DAT recording made from Disklavier play-back
Producer: Richard Riley
Engineer: Richard Riley
Cover: PianoMania
Notes: Max Morath

Drugstore Cabaret (Piano/Vocals)
Custom recording produced for the American Institute of the History of Pharmacy, for the American Pharmaceutical Assn., underwritten by Searle, Inc.
Cassette only, in vinyl book package, with booklet notes by   Allen G. Debus
Recorded at Fox Studios, Rutherford NJ
Project Director: Robert A. Buerki
Producer: Normacks, Inc.
Engineers: David Blake, Jeff Zaraya
Album Design: Robert A. Buerki
Cover Art: Al Hirschfeld

1992 The Ragtime Man (Piano Solos)
Omega (3013); CD only
This is a reissue of "Cripple Creek—A Ragtime Suite for Piano" and "Best of Ragtime Piano" originally issued on cassette by Mel Bay Publications (see above, 1986)
Digital Remastering: David Baker
Art Director: Fred Holtz
Cover Photo: Martha Swope

1993 Siren Songs (Ann Fennessy, soprano; piano accompaniment Max Morath)
Bilnan productions (BN 1021); CD only
Recorded and produced in Spokane, WA
Executive Producer: William Hursh
Producer: Robert Curnow
Engineer: Michael Wagner
Cover & Design: Bassett & Brush Studios
Photography: Rick Singer

1994 Real American Folk Songs (Vocal/Piano)
SoloArt, a label of Jazzology/GHB, New Orleans (SACD-120); CD only
Recorded at Seltzer Sound Studios, New York
Producers: Max Morath, George Buck
Engineer: Carl Seltzer
Cover Photo: John McCormack

REISSUES

The Ragtime Women
Vanguard-Welk (79402); CD and CS
As above

Fountain Favorites
Coca-Cola special project: CD & CS
New cover design

A Ragtime Primer (Vol. I) (Piano Solos, with other artists)
PianoMania (123); CD only
Includes three solos, reissued from "The Ragtime Century" (above)
Producer: Richard Riley
Notes: Richard Zimmerman
Cover Photo: Graphi-Cat Printing

Drugstore Cabaret: Songs about Sodas, Pills and Potions (Vocal/Piano)
Premier (1050); CD only
Reissue of "Drugstore Cabaret" cassette (above)
Producer for Premier: Bob Stern
Remastering: Jeff Zaraya
Art Director: Eugene Rowley and Charles Sands
Cover Photo: American Institute of the History of Pharmacy

1996 REISSUES

Don't Give the Name Bad Place (Vocals with Piano & Quartet)
New World (80265); CD only
Reissue of LP (above)
Digital remastering: Paul Zinman, Soundbyte Productions, New York

Jonah Man—A Tribute to Bert Williams
Vanguard-Welk (79378); CD & CS
LP (above) in reissue; minor change in subtitle
Four instrumental tracks (rags) added to original LP vocal tracks, from "Ragtime Stompers" (1981)

1997 A Century of Ragtime ñ 1897–1997 (Piano Solos)
Vanguard (Welk Music Group) 167/68); Two CD set
Pianos solos by various artists, licensed from various
labels; CD #2 is orchestral
Issued on the 100th Anniversary of the first publica-
tion of ragtime in 1897
Producers: Bonnie Pritchard & Richard Zimmerman
Digital Remastering: Jeff Zaraya
Design: Unicorn Publishing Services

REISSUE

Living a Ragtime Life (Vocal/Piano)
Normacks (101A); cassette only
Remastered to confirm to content of SoloArt CD, above
Digital remastering: Zomax, Inc., Minneapolis

*Yet another reuse of "Living a Ragtime Life." When it came time
to reorder the 1987 cassette version of this album, we decided to
bring it up to the same contents as the SoloArt CD version, which
added five numbers, and also decided to resequence the music.
This is the same material as SoloArt's "Living a Ragtime Life," (or
LARL, as we call it,) but in a different order. We even changed the
cover from white to pink, to match the CD—and the video.*

*SHOULD A VIDEO BE LISTED IN A DISCOGRAPHY? YES, IF
YOU HAVE ONLY ONE VIDEO—HARDLY ENOUGH FOR A
SECTION CALLED "VIDEOGRAPHY." THIS VIDEO IS A
RESPONSE TO FOLKS WHO WANT THE MONOLOGS AND
COMEDY, ALONG WITH THE RAGS AND SONGS, MOST OF
WHICH ARE ALSO AVAILABLE ON THE AUDIO RECORD-
INGS.*

VIDEO 1997

Living A Ragtime Life (Piano/Vocals/Monologs)
Normacks, Inc. (No #); VHS; running time 75 minutes
The one-man show, taped before in live performance at
Denver Media Center, Denver, Colorado
Producer: Max Morath, for Normacks, Inc.
Executive Producer: Steve Delano, Denver Media
Center
Post-Production: Juntunen Video, Minneapolis
Video Editor: Joe Palo
Packaging and Design: Laura Cobb, Vaughn Group,
Minneapolis
Cover Art: Al Hirschfeld

*AND WHAT ABOUT PIANO ROLLS? I HAVEN'T MADE
ENOUGH TO QUALITY FOR A FULL-SCALE
"ROLLOGRAPHY," SO SINCE IT'S JUST ANOTHER WAY FOR
RECORDING PIANO SOLOS, I FIGURED WE COULD
APPEND IT HERE, ALONG WITH THE VIDEO.*

ROLLOGRAPHY

QRS Music Rolls Inc., Buffalo, New York
Session: August 23, 1974, at QRS (hand-played in
real time)
Selections: *The Entertainer, Scott Joplin's New Rag,
Cottontail Rag, Easy Winners, Grace and Beauty,
Polyragmic*
Ramsi P. Tick, QRS President
Brian A. Williams, Vice President
These rolls were released during 1975–1976 and
remain in QRS catalog.

The Compositions

This is a fairly complete list of the piano rags and songs I've composed over the years. Also listed are my adaptations, rewrites, and arrangements of songs and rags from the Ragtime Years, with the original composer(s) names attached. Most items on this list are currently in print or available through libraries and collectors.

Symbols for publishers, agents, and societies are as follows:

H/TRO: Hollis Music/the Richmond Organization, New York, N.Y.
EBM: Edward B. Marks Music, New York, N.Y.
CRM: Cherry River Music, Port Chester, New York
MBP: Mel Bay Publications, Pacific, Missouri
DEG: Deganawidah Music, Astoria, New York
BMI: Broadcast Music, Inc. Performing Society, New York, N.Y.

Adaptations (adp) Arrangements (arr)

ANCHORIA LELAND (A RAG) (Piano) MBP.1981, 1986. CRM. 1993. *Cripple Creek Suite.* (DEG)

BOSTON CAKEWALK, THE (Song) Fred Stone. H/TRO. 1963. (adp)

BRASS RING, THE (Brass quintet) EBM. 1983, 1986.

BULL FROG SONG, THE (Song) Chas. E. Trevathan. H/TRO. 1964. (adp)

CAKEWALKIN' JAMBOREE (Song/piano) H/TRO. 1964. (adp)

CAKEWALKIN' SHOES (Song) H/TRO. 1964.

DOCTOR JACKPOT (Piano) MBP. 1986. CRM. 1993. *Cripple Creek Suite.* (DEG)

DORIANNA (Song) H. Von Tilzer/Andrew Sterling. H/TRO. 1964. (adp)

EASY WINNERS (Piano) Scott Joplin. H/TRO. 1964. (simplified arr)

ECHOES OF THE CAKEWALK (Piano) H/TRO. 1964. (original/adp)

ECHOES OF THE ROSEBUD (Piano) H/TRO. 1976. (new material & adp)

ELISA, LISTEN (Song) EBM. 1976.

ELITE SYNCOPATIONS (Song/Piano) new w. & m. based on a Scott Joplin rag. Unpublished. 1990.

ENTERTAINER, THE (Song/Piano) new w. & m. based on a Scott Joplin rag. Unpublished. 1990. (DEG)

FIVE DERIVED (Piano) Unpublished. 1984.

GOLD BAR RAG (Piano) H/TRO. 1956, 1964.

GOLDEN HOURS, THE (Piano) H/TRO. 1966, 1972.

HELLO RAGTIME (Song/Piano) new w. & m. based on a Scott Joplin rag. Unpublished. 1990.

HONEST JOHN RILEY (Song) Edw. Harrigan/Dave Braham. H/TRO. 1964. (adp)

HONEY, WILL YOU MISS ME? (Song) Howard & Emerson. H/TRO. 1964. (adp)

I GOT TO LIVE ANYHOW 'TIL I DIE (Song) Shepard N. Edmonds. EBM. 1976. (adp)

IF YOU DON'T HAVE ANY MONEY (THE MONEY SONG) Clarence S. Brewster & A. B. Sloane. H/TRO. 1964. (adp)

IMPERIAL RAG (Piano) 1954, 1982. MBP. 1986. CRM. 1993. *Cripple Creek Suite.* (DEG)

IN SEPARATE ROOMS (Song cycle w/piano) w. Emily Dickinson, music by Max Morath. Based on rag themes by Scott Joplin. Unpublished. 1990, 1997. (DEG)

IT'S MOVING DAY (Song) H. Von Tilzer/Andrew Sterling. H/TRO. 1964. (adp)

JONAH MAN (Song) Alex Rogers & Bert Williams. EBM. 1976. (adp)

KERRY CAKEWALK (Song/Piano) Kerry Mills. H/TRO. 1964. (adp)

MA BLUSHIN' ROSIE (Song) Edgar Smith/John Stromberg. H/TRO. 1964. (arr)

MY LOU (Song) Dave Augustin. H/TRO Music. 1964. (arr)

MY CREOLE BELLE (Song/Piano) J. Bodewalt Lampe. H/TRO. 1964. (adp)

NEW BLACK EAGLE BUCK, THE (Piano) EBM. 1976.

OH, MISTER JOHNSON (Song) Ben Harney. H/TRO. 1963. (adp & arr)

OLD MORTALITY (SLOW DRAG) (Piano) MBP. 1986. CRM. 1993. *Cripple Creek Suite.* (DEG)

ONE FOR AMELIA (Piano) H/TRO. 1964.

ONE FOR NORMA (Piano) EBM. 1976.

ONE FOR THE ROAD (Piano) EBM. 1982. (Band arr. J. Tatgenhorst)

PIANO ROLLIN' RAG (Piano) H/TRO. 1969. (adp)

POLYRAGMIC (Piano) H/TRO. 1964.

POVERTY GULCH (A Ragtime Two-Step) (Piano) MBP. 1986. CRM. 1993. *Cripple Creek Suite* (DEG)

RAGTIME'S THE RIGHT TIME (Song) new words, based on a song by Roger Lewis & Ernie Erdman. Unpublished. 1991.

RAW GIN (Song) unpublished. 1958.

SAVE IT FOR ME (Song) Bob Cole/J. W. Johnson. EBM. 1964, 1976. (adp)

SOMEBODY'S THINKING OF YOU (Song) m. Gladys R. Morath. Unpublished. 1996.

TEMPORARY BABY (Song) H/TRO. 1977.

TENNESSEE SYNCOPES (Piano) Charles Hunter. H/TRO. 1964. (adp)

THREE FOR DIANE (Piano) unpublished. 1994.

TRIBUTE TO JOPLIN (Piano) themes by Scott Joplin. H/TRO. 1964. (adp)

VINDICATOR RAG (Piano) 1958. MBP. 1986. CRM. 1993. *Cripple Creek Suite.* (DEG)

WHEN IT'S ALL GOIN' OUT AND NOTHIN' COMIN' IN (Song) Bert Williams & George Walker. EBM. 1976.

Credits

All photographs are by Diane Fay Skomars except the following:

Opposite "Introductions": Richard Olsenius, courtesy Minneapolis/St. Paul *Tribune*.

In "The Entertainer": (source of many of the photographs is unknown)

Page Number	Photographer
24	Diane Fay Skomars
29	Jack P. Shoup
32	Cripple Creek *Times-Record*
33	Knutsen-Bowers
34 (lower right)	C. M. "Bud" Edmonds
34 (upper right)	Dick Hill
35–37	Knutsen-Bowers
38, 39	Don Allen
40	John W. Ripley
43	Don Allen
50–51	Van Williams
53	Fred Moldenhauer
59	Ken Howard
60, 61 (lower)	Diane Fay Skomars
62, 63 (lower right)	Diane Fay Skomars
63 (lower left)	Steve Goodman

BLAKE & SISSLE PHOTO (with "Thinking about the Music")
From *Reminiscing with Sissle and Blake*. Kimball & Bolcom. Viking, 1973.

CDs, audio and video tapes, and additional copies
of this book may be ordered from:

LARSMONT, INC.
100 Glen Road
Woodcliff Lake, N.J. 07675
(FAX 201-476-9052)

www.maxmorath.com

ONE FOR THE ROAD

Piano Solo

By
MAX MORATH

2